Bunty &
Best wishes
Kevin McCusker.

Sectarian Birkenhead

by Kevin McCusker

For Patrick and Terry. Perhaps now you will read the bloody thing.

CONTENTS

Chapter One - 4

Chapter Two - 28

Chapter Three - 41

Chapter Four - 66

Chapter Five - 79

Chapter Six - 96

Chapter Seven - 117

Chapter Eight - 166

Chapter Nine - 185

Chapter Ten - 190

CHAPTER ONE

Birkenhead: City of the Future?

This book will describe the origins of sectarian politics in Birkenhead. The practitioners of sectarianism targeted Irish Catholics, with the intention of excluding them from respectable society and keeping them as a submerged underclass. It will show how John Laird was co-opted into sectarian politics, not so difficult a task given his Orange background. It will also show how the Birkenhead Garibaldi riots of 1862 can be seen as an episode in the development of a sectarian Conservative Party, which hung onto power until well into the 20th century in Birkenhead, as it did in Liverpool also.

In the 1840s Britain was the world's superpower; its industrial and financial centre. British entrepreneurs were changing the face of the world. Iron, steam, and enterprise were enabling British superiority over all other nations. British merchants, capitalists and railway builders were promoted as heroes. They were compared to legendary Tudors, such as Cardinal Wolsey and Henry VIII, or even the ancient Alexander the Great.

For many, Birkenhead was the very symbol of the age. Relatively few individuals had mobilised large sums of capital to build a completely new town. What follows is an article from The Chambers Edinburgh Review of 1845. The writer had visited the new town in the making.

A VISIT TO BIRKENHEAD

A time of vast mechanical means like the present has its sublimities as well as the earlier ages of the world. A Liverpool millionaire said one day not long ago to a meeting of Perthshire proprietors, 'Unless you do so and so, I'll take my railway by the east of Fife.' Consider what a railway is, and say if Wolsey's 'Ego et Rex' (Myself and the King), was a grander thing for a subject to speak than this? About the same time, another great railway hero - a man who a few years since was a shopkeeper in York - was commissioned by a set of brother directors to accomplish a particular object for the general interest, and two million were placed at his disposal for the purpose. 'Take that sum', they told him, 'and make the best of it.' Alexander's passage of the Granicus with a handful of hardy Greeks was no doubt a fine thing, but there is as much of the grand, in its own way, in what many English merchants are doing every day. Talk of utility as having overpowered the poetical with us! On the contrary, the world has never seen or known a poetry like what a right spirit can trace in hundreds of the facts by which we are now surrounded.

One of the facts which has most deeply impressed us lately, is the sudden rise of a new city in England. A city we are accustomed to consider as the growth of centuries, for cities heretofore have always taken centuries to build. But now, such is the hugeness of the power created by the industry and wealth of this country, there is at least one city which will undoubtedly have risen within the brief space between the boyhood and manhood of its first inhabitants. We allude to Birkenhead on the Mersey, near Liverpool. By far the greater number of our readers will never have heard of this place even by name; yet it is one or the greatest wonders of the age, and indeed one of those by which the character of our age is most strongly expressed. We visited it lately in order to ascertain how far the reports about it were true, and we now propose conveying to the public some idea of what we saw and learned on the spot.

The Mersey at Liverpool is a river or estuary, two thirds of a mile in breadth. The ground opposite to the great emporium of commerce was, till a recent period, altogether waste, or occupied by farms or hamlets. One of the latter, named Birkenhead, had risen in connection with a priory of the eleventh century. Steam navigation at length facilitating the intercourse between the two sides of the river, the sloping banks opposite Liverpool had become crested by a few ranges of neat mansions for the merchants of that town, and thus things went on till two or three years ago. A few enterprising persons then became aware of a creek in the river at Birkenhead, for commercial purposes and proposed converting it into a set of docks, supplementary to the mighty range covering six miles in connection with their own town. The Corporation of Liverpool had bought the land surrounding Wallasey Pool, as this creek was called, for £180,000, and now they were not unwilling to transfer their purchase. It was bought and Parliament applied to, for permission to lay out £400,000 in the formation of the proposed docks. At the same time, a city capable of containing a hundred thousand inhabitants is rising, which our posterity will yet know as familiarly as we do now Liverpool itself, or any other of the large towns of Britain.

Our visit to Birkenhead took place on a sunny April morning of the present year. Landing from the steamers, which cross the Mersey every half hour, we walked into this City of the Future with expectations which the reality by no means disappointed. When we had passed a mere frontier of short streets overlooking the river, we were at once launched into a miles breadth of street building where unfinished houses, unmade roadways, brickfields, scaffolding, heaps of mortar, loaded wains and troops of workmen meet the eye in every direction, It was like the scene which Virgil describes when he introduces Aeneas and his companion into Carthage, but like nothing which has ever met our eyes in real life. where houses were occupied or shops opened, they all had a peculiarly fresh, sparkling look, like furniture in an upholsterer's wareroom as compared to that in private dwellings. The very children walking or playing in the streets looked old beside them. In some streets, traceable as such by buildings posted here and there along a line, the substratum of the roadway was only in the course of being formed; in others the process had advanced as far as the superficies of macadamized trap, but hardly anywhere was a beaten and smoother road to be seen. You entered a piece of street with a particular name, and half an hour after, walking in quite a different part of the country, for country it still is in some measure, you fall into another piece of street bearing the same name. You wonder at first, but presently it appears they are various extremities on one street, only there is a wild wilderness of brickfields between them. You ask for the public buildings and find they are all in the masons' hands, excepting a few churches. There is to be a capital town hall, a capital market, a capital everything. We looked into the market, and found the walls and ceiling formed; a vast hall (430 by 131 ft), supported by light iron pillars, and lighted from the roof.

Birkenhead Market[1]

The business going on while we were there was the laying down of the gas-pipes. Nearby is the grand square of Birkenhead - a subject of pride with the inhabitants, as it happens there is nothing approaching it in spaciousness or elegance in Liverpool. But probably from being spoiled by the beauties of our own fair city, we thought Hamilton Square no more than passable; nor did the interior of the houses make up in elegance or comfort, for a somewhat poor kind of architecture.

Making a detour towards the east, we found a beautiful slope rising above the nascent town and occupied by a fine range of villas scattered throughout its space. This is Clifton Park, and it comprehends an arrangement which we have often thought might be followed with advantage in every large town in the empire. The principle is, that the

---

1 Illustrated London News, April 3, 1847

place is an ornamented piece of ground, which both generally and in its parts as the usual recommendation of pleasure ground, while houses are only scattered over it, each having the command of a certain space without interfering with the general arrangements for walks, or with the general effect from a distance. That every family may be said to have the advantage of neighbourhood combined with the delices of a fine rural situation.

After a considerable walk, we reached the part of the environs which is calculated to make a greater impression than perhaps any other thing connected with the town. The misfortune of all ordinary large towns is that they have to struggle with difficulties imposed by former centuries: narrow streets, the nuisance of cemeteries, the want of right sewerage and of places of recreation for the inhabitants. Here Birkenhead, being a town building from the foundation in an enlightened age, has a great advantage. Its sewerage may be perfect if the managers choose; and it will be their eternal disgrace if this essential point be overlooked or inadequately attended to. They need have no lanes, no cul de sacs, no courts, none of the architectural curses of Liverpool. Finally, they have it in their power to reserve part of the ground at their command for recreation. We feel the greatest pleasure in stating that, following the improved sanitary reviews of the last few years, they have made it one of their first cares to establish a 'park' - meaning thereby an open piece of ornamented ground - for the future inhabitants of their city. We found it in the course of being formed under the direction of the well-known Mr Paxton of Chatsworth; and to judge from what we saw of it in rather unfavourable circumstances, it promises to be a fine place. The space to be operated upon was a hundred and eighty acres, sixty being set apart for building purposes, there remain a hundred and twenty to be laid out in shrubberies, walks, and drives. Remembering what has been made of the eleven acres given by Mr Strutt to the people of Derby, we cannot doubt that a quantity eleven times greater will fulfil the objects of the managers most amply. Already the required undulations of the ground have been affected; vast quantities of trees and flowers have been planted; two sheets of water are formed; several lodges are built; and though the act of purchasing the ground dates only from September last, we may be said to have the first sketch of a park presented to our eyes. The whole is expected to be complete and at the service of the public next September. We were delighted with what we saw here, but the satisfaction of the eye is nothing in such a case; the point really to be rejoiced in, is that the ideas of men are so far advanced, with respect to the essentials of public health and conveniency, that, in preparing a new city, a park for the use of the inhabitants should have been among the first things legislated for. To the same advancement is it to be attributed that the ground set apart for burying the future inhabitants of Birkenhead is at a spot called Flaybrick Hill, which also will be out of town. Here excavations are in progress for the construction of sepulchral vaults and catacombs, the removed stone being used - for the managers, like Mrs Gilpin, are of a frugal mind - in the formation of the docks. The slaughterhouses are also out of town - a suite of buildings properly enclosed and supplied with every requisite for the preservation of cleanliness and order. Birkenhead will teach many useful lessons to older towns, and this is one of them.

We came at last to the docks, which are formed by the simple process of sluicing the water of the Wallasey Pool and building quays along its banks. The inner dock will be of 150 acres in extent, with 19 ft depth of water; and there will be an outer or low water harbour of 37 acres, with quay space of 300 ft in breadth (reclaimed from the sea) on each side. A range of warehouses will front the wet docks on the side towards the town. Besides these accommodations for shipping, there will be a small dock of 3 acres, and a tidal basin of 16, with beaching ground for coasting vessels. There will thus be provided, on the Cheshire side of the Mersey, a range of docks containing an area of 206 acres. Such a work undertaken and produced at once, may safely be pronounced without parallel in this country. Around the site of the proposed docks are already various important works. There is a large establishment for the construction of iron vessels, and at which many have been built. There is also a varnish manufacturer, an iron foundry, a patent slip for repairing vessels, and a boiler yard.

We found three ferries between various points of Liverpool and Birkenhead, the fare two- pence. It is not unworthy of notice that the receipts are higher at that small rate than when it was double the sum. It is designed ere long to have steamers plying between the two shores every five minutes, which will certainly be making a near approach to the conveniency of a bridge. From one landing place on the Birkenhead side, a railway starts for Chester, where it is continued by another line to a point on the Grand Junction, and thus brought in union with the principal ways of this kind in the kingdom. The mails from London to Dublin are conveyed by this route, and it is commonly used by parties passing between the Irish and English capitals. The steamer passes from Kingston near Dublin to Birkenhead in about 10 hours, and from thence the mail-train will convey passengers to London in about the same time. It is also contemplated to have a railway to Manchester, a ship canal to connect the Mersey and the Dee, and various other great works.

> It may be inquired how far Birkenhead is a built and inhabited town, and the answer is, that the actual population a few months ago was found to be about 15000. In 1823, it was a few hundred, and probably in 10 years it will be approaching 100,000. Land which a few years ago hardly possessed a value, is now selling £6 a square yard, and by good speculations in that line, large fortunes have been acquired. We now take leave of the subject, with best wishes for the success of Birkenhead. Of the probabilities of that success we say not a word; but we feel assured that, if the contemplated work shall be duly completed, the banks of the Mersey will present the grandest monument which the 19th century has erected to the genius of commerce and peace.[2]

So it was, with a spirit of boundless optimism and enthusiastic publicity, that the promoters of Birkenhead approached the year 1847. That was the year of the unveiling of the 'City of the Future'. It was to prove a year first of triumph and then of tragedy.

Another glory on the Mersey's side,
A town springs up as from a magic wand,
Behold these noble docks – the merchants' pride,
And the fair park extending o'er the Strand.
The gallant bark that often had defied
The wild Atlantic may no longer dread
The treacherous shores; in safety now 'twill ride
Within the waters of fair Birkenhead.
Good, great, and glorious is the work. The bond
A brotherhood between two worlds, hereby
Is made more closely: and affection freed

---

2 The Chambers Edinburgh Review, 17th May, 1845

Will spring up where before frown'd enmity.
Process to Birkenhead – the commerce, trade
And may true worth the people's hearts pervade.[3]

Opening of the Dock[4]

[3] Illustrated London News, April 14th, 1847, p.228

[4] Ibid

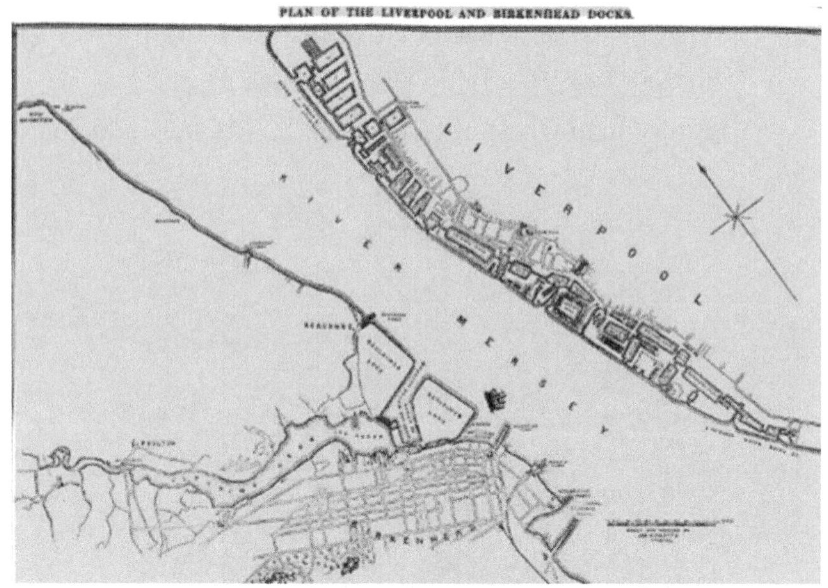

Plan of the Liverpool and Birkenhead Docks[5]

First consider the events of 1847, a crucial year in Birkenhead's development. The year began on a tide of optimism for the future of the town. On Easter Monday, 5th April, 1847, several huge projects, years in the making, had a grand gala opening.

A dock, which was opened by Lord Morpeth, was the first instalment of a much grander scheme, in which the whole of Wallasey Pool was to be converted into quays.

According to the Liverpool Mercury, this grand scheme was first proposed by John Laird's father, William, in the 1820s. William had commissioned Thomas Telford to survey the site and Telford had approved Laird's plan. However, Liverpool Corporation, wary of competition, had proceeded to buy up the land surrounding the Pool. They spent about £100,000 in 1847 prices, many millions in today's money. The Birkenhead Dock Company, of which John Laird, and his brother William, were directors, bought the land back for £250,000 in 1843. It was envisaged that the whole scheme would be finished by late 1847.

---

[5] Plan of Docks, Liverpool Mercury, 6th April 1847, p. 4

The Illustrated London News also publicised the events, and forecast a splendid future for the town:

> On Monday last a portion of the immense docks was opened with the éclat befitting such an important incident, and a vast concourse of persons assembled to witness the ceremony. The works thrown open formed but a small part of this magnificent and comprehensive scheme, but what has already been accomplished gives a goodly promise of a speedy completion of a most useful and efficient set of docks, the promoters of which may hope, at no very distant day, to see them, on account of their extensive usefulness, worthy of being associated with those on the other side of the Mersey. Birkenhead may be said to have entered into competition, or rather into articles of partnership, with Liverpool, the great north outlet and inlet of our transatlantic trade. At any rate, it will henceforth divide the palm with Liverpool, and participate in the prosperity and profit derivable from its immense mercantile marine. Birkenhead may fairly be looked upon as if of Liverpool lineage and alliance, and to literally having been called into life by that Leviathan of trade itself in its effort towards finding an ampler field for the accommodation and convenience of its ever- grown trade. Birkenhead will become a sort of chapel of ease for the redundant commerce of the mother port, and probably there is no port in the kingdom, not excepting Liverpool itself, that presents such grand natural facilities. A few years hence, and Birkenhead will become a second Liverpool launched upon the Mersey; for time was when, at the beginning of the eighteenth century, Liverpool itself, now the entrepot of all our trade with the Americas and the Indies, was simply a fishing village. The same a few years hence may be said of Birkenhead. Both are probably the finest example on record of the brilliant results of

unfettered British enterprise. Anciently, the settlement and consolidation of a town was the work of generations. Now, thanks to steam, they spring up and prosper with all the rapidity of the famed ice palace of the Queen of Russia. Great advantage may be expected to accrue to the public and frequenters from foreign ports from the generous emulation that will be established between the old and new ports, and in a few years the northern, no less that the eastern arm of the Mersey, may be expected to be the seat of a crowded and busy community. It will give no insignificant idea of the immenseness of Liverpool, that it extends for three miles along the Mersey and is upward of a mile in breadth. Liverpool has for years had at her command a comprehensive and splendid chain of railways, and unsurpassed port facilities. Upon these Birkenhead is only just entering. Monday gave England, in the latter respect, a new port of ingress and egress to the Western seas; but Birkenhead will have to wait awhile for the completion of her railways. It is true she has long had one, but this is less than half what she wants. Ere long she will be the very 'rosette' of railways, for in addition to the existing Chester and Birkenhead, she will have the Birkenhead, Lancashire and Cheshire Junction, operations on which have just been commenced by the contractors in real earnest, and in addition to drawing all the commerce of the manufacturing district to the Mersey, will give to Birkenhead the mineral trade of Wales, the salt traffic of Cheshire, the immense products of the Potteries, besides having with Holyhead the traffic to Ireland. If Rome was not built in a day, Birkenhead, by a figure of speech, assuredly has been. We have in it a great mercantile community, with all its moral and commercial apparatus springing remorselessly and almost magically into action under the vivifying power of English enterprise. We have it put in

> possession, at the same time, of docks for forests of foreign masts, with warehouses for living their wares and with a railway for their transit to inland homes.[6]

A festival committee had been appointed to organise a grand dinner and ball with four hundred guests invited. Notable for their absence were the Mayor of Liverpool and the Chairman of the Dock Committee. The Liverpool Mercury attributed this to a "petty feeling of jealousy".

The Illustrated London News article could have been written as a prospectus for the four official bodies involved in the projects, namely the Commissioners for Birkenhead, the Birkenhead Dock Company, the Chester and Birkenhead Railway and the Birkenhead, Cheshire, and Lancashire Junction Railway Company. They were a vision of the future for the companies. But there were also plans for the town as a whole.

When William Laird came to the village of Birkenhead in 1824, he had radical visions of the future. William came from Scotland and had been enormously impressed by Edinburgh's New Town, and especially by the Moray Estate, designed to house Scotland's elite. He commissioned the architects of that estate, James Gillespie Graham, to plan the proposed new town of Birkenhead. Hamilton Square and the broad, straight streets leading from it were the product of his design. The square itself was composed of elegant villas for the "mercantile community" of Birkenhead and Liverpool, since the ferry was a few minutes' walk away.

---

[6] Illustrated London News, April 10th, 1847, p. 227

Opening of the Birkenhead Docks and Park[7]

In 1841 the Improvement Commission, very much influenced by the Lairds' vision of Birkenhead, had approved the spending of public money on building the world's first public park.

The park cost a great deal of money, £125,000. It was designed by Joseph Paxton, the country's leading landscape architect. The park was intended to be self- financing, surrounded by the sort of elegant villas already being built in Hamilton Square. It was to be a magnet for the mercantile community which would commute to Liverpool or be based in the second Liverpool that Birkenhead would become. It would be a picturesque backdrop for elegant living for merchants and their families, and an alternative to the alehouse for the workers.

[7] Ibid, p. 10

Opening of the Birkenhead Docks and Park[8]

John Laird's dreams for Birkenhead were not confined to the middle classes. He also had housing built for workers on his schemes. Model housing for the working classes was becoming fashionable in some upper-class circles, it was a cause taken up by Prince Albert.

> DWELLINGS FOR THE WORKING CLASSES
> The attention which is now being paid by the richer classes to the physical wants, the social and domestic comforts, and, consequently, the moral and intellectual advancement of the humbler and labouring portion of society, is one of the distinctive and most pleasing characteristics of the present day. ... In Liverpool much is doing, or is about to be done, in the right direction: but if we cross the Mersey and take a walk through Birkenhead, we find much that

8 Ibid p. 10

> has been done. The public parks, the wide streets, the attention to drainage and sewage, all bespeak an attention and foresight much to be commended; but the cottages built by the Birkenhead Dock Company, for the residences of the work men, will long remain as monuments of the commencement of a new era, which, we trust, will bring with it health, happiness, ay, and comparative wealth to the industrious people of this country. The buildings are erected on the plan of the houses in Scotland, each tenant occupying a 'flat', and, as they are four stories in height, eight families are accommodated in each house. Most of the cottages consist of three apartments, a kitchen and two bedrooms. The kitchen is fitted up with a grate, oven, etc. ... We are confident that all who take the least interest in the welfare and improvement of the working classes will feel gratified by a personal inspection of 'The Workman's Cottages'.[9]

In 1850 Punch magazine printed two cartoons, showing the contrast between the sober respectability resulting from the provision of decent accommodation, and the vice which resulted from the conditions in which workers lived, in the explosively growing industrial towns in Britain. Unfortunately for the people of Birkenhead and Laird's dream of a model town filled with handsome dwellings, much of the town's housing came to resemble the picture of the cellar dwellings. The boom of early 1847 was followed by the bust of late 1847 and an influx of impoverished and starving Irish people, overwhelmingly Catholic.

---

[9] Ibid, p. 10

The Model Lodging-House[10]

The Cellar[11]

---

[10] Punch Almanac 1850, Published at The Office, 85 Fleet Street, London

The Birkenhead Dock Cottages[12]

The boom was a product of investment in, and construction of railways, in which Birkenhead played more than its fair share. Railways had been immensely profitable at first and investors had been very willing to earn high returns. By the mid-1840s dozens of lines were being constructed around the country. People were encouraged to invest by reading the sort of puffery quoted earlier by the Illustrated London News about Birkenhead's future. It soon became clear that some of the lines would never be profitable. The value of shares in railways collapsed in late 1847, as did shares in property associated with them, Birkenhead's Dock Company included. By October 1847, it was apparent that the Dock Company was in financial crisis. Who could help them out? A letter appeared in the

---

[11] Ibid

[12] The Birkenhead Dock Cottages, hiddenwirral.org 2014, viewed 23rd July 2020

Liverpool Mercury:

> PROPOSED SALE OF THE BIRKENHEAD DOCKS
>
> Gentlemen, - I see by the papers that a negotiation is actually on foot for the sale of these docks to the Liverpool Dock Trust; and no doubt the Birkenhead Dock Warehouse interest will keep company. When that sale is effected, the death-knell of Birkenhead is rung; mark the prophecy.
>
> How the mighty have fallen! but yesterday Liverpool lay prostrate before Birkenhead ... today, Birkenhead licks the hand that wounded, and would have slain; she kisses the rod with all becoming humility. ... To those who are interested in the welfare of Birkenhead it is distressing to see such mismanagement. ... The parties to benefit by the sale are the bondholders and the Dock Warehouse Company, and also the owners of private warehouses in Liverpool; while the entire population of Birkenhead, owners of property, ratepayers, and all classes who have had the misfortune to invest their property or their bodies within its bounds; the commercial people of Liverpool, and the general consuming body there, and also the manufacturing districts will be injured.
>
> Of all the suicidal acts of which the present Birkenhead authorities have been guilty ... that now under consideration is the most fatal. Can they shut their eyes to the fact that in selling their docks they are literally selling their country - the country which was placed in their hands for safekeeping?[13]

Two months later the Mercury ran a story:

> In 1843, a great want of dock accommodation existed in the Mersey; Liverpool had then only 100 acres of

[13] Liverpool Mercury, Oct 19th 1847, p. 3

> dock room, and that space was much incommoded by the bulky and increasing trades of timber, cotton, grain etc. To remedy this the Birkenhead scheme was proposed, affording great extent of accommodation at a very low figure. To compete with this project the Liverpool Dock Trustees brought forward a plan for making eighty additional acres of docks at the North End of the town. Parliament sanctioned both schemes, and it was now an even race which side of the water should get to work first. The Birkenhead commissioners got the money too easily, perhaps; instead of the works being completed for £400,000, the original estimate, they awoke one morning to the disagreeable truth that £1,000,000 would be required. Confidence was shaking, and the race lost. The Liverpool Dock Trustees, on this, redoubled their energy, pressed on their works, and will have 80 acres of docks open in the summer of 1848, while Birkenhead has only 7! The Warehouse Company has thus, through the want of energy on the part of the Birkenhead Commissioners, and the erroneous calculations of the engineer, lost its chance; the splendid workhouses, after eight months trial, have only received some three or four cargoes - every inducement has been tried to coax trade - low charges - a free dock - and no dues on goods; but all have failed I think, therefore, the proprietors have come to a wise decision in determining to wind up the concern.[14]

Mortimer had published *The History of the Hundred of Wirral,* in 1847. His description of Birkenhead consists largely of praise for the enterprise of the promoters of the town, like Williams Jackson and the Laird brothers, and the wonders they had built, but tacked on, almost as an afterthought, is a description of the town in late 1847. It tells a tale, essentially, of speculation gone bad.

---

[14] Liverpool Mercury, 7th Dec, 1847, p. 8

> It is, however, difficult to predict concerning the future of Birkenhead: events of the next few years may affect a great alteration in the town, which is at present, beyond all doubt, in a state of great depression. From the evidence given before the Surveying Officers ... on the Gas and Water Bills ... it appeared there were 2,702 occupied houses; no less than 893 uninhabited, exclusive of 444 unfinished.[15]

The population of Birkenhead in 1841 was 8,223, in 1851 it was 24,285. There had evidently been a great deal of migration into the town but the overall figures disguise what Mortimer attests to – many skilled workers had left the town and sought opportunities elsewhere. Mortimer continues:

> It cannot be denied that there has been too great, too rapid an influx into Birkenhead, which until it can earn money of its own, from imports or manufactures, or from both, must be considered as a suburb of Liverpool, and a place of residence for those whose means of living are drawn from that great town.[16]

The continued expansion of John Laird's shipyard and the arrival of Thomas Brassey's railway-building Canada Works were to provide that basis of industry in the 1860s, but the dream of Birkenhead as a great port to rival Liverpool was gone.

Worries about depopulation were not to last long. Instead, Birkenhead was faced with an influx of largely unwelcome immigrants from Ireland. 1847 was perhaps the worst year of the Irish Famine. A new Liberal Government decided on a change of policy in Ireland. Government intervention in Ireland was to be reduced. The Liberal

---

15 Mortimer William Williams, The History of The Hundred of Wirral: With a Sketch of the City and County of Chester Whitaker &Company Cheshire, 1847, p. 437, p. 438

16 Ibid, p. 438

Party was now largely the party of the industrial/financial middle classes. They decided that their class enemy, the aristocracy, were responsible for the famine, through mismanagement of their Irish estates. Irish landowners were now to pay for the upkeep of the starving. Landowners were to pay poor rates on their tenants' holdings. Many landowners responded by simply evicting their tenants. People were evicted and their homes rendered uninhabitable.

The result was that parts of Ireland became an open-air concentration camp. Crowds of ragged, starving people wandered aimlessly, living, and dying without shelter. It was estimated that a million died, either of hunger or typhus fever. A million and a half emigrated, most of them through Liverpool. Those with money went to America, those with a little stayed in Liverpool or went to Birkenhead, those without starved. Mortimer wrote:

> Numbers, immediately after their arrival in Liverpool, crossed the Mersey to Birkenhead; some on pretence of seeking employment, others travelling into the interior, but, in almost every instance, with an intention to beg. Proceeding direct to the parish offices – principally women and children – were so great, their applications for food so urgent, and their destitution so apparent, that the ordinary laws of vagrancy were suspended, or rather defeated.[17]

Once the initial crisis was over, the Poor Law Authorities resumed the practice of returning Irish people applying for poor relief to their home parishes in Ireland, as the New Poor Law entitled them to do. The results were predictable, as the Liverpool Mercury reported:

> DEATHS FROM STARVATION: DISTRESSING OCCURRENCE AT BIRKENHEAD.
>
> It is this week our sad duty to record two deaths, resulting, there is every reason to fear, from starvation. On Sunday afternoon, in consequence of information received, Inspector McNeill proceeded to

[17] Ibid, p. 438

an empty house in Oak Street, Birkenhead, where he found a woman lying dead upon the floor, and a child, about nine months old, also dead, lying at her feet. Four young children, whose ages average from about four to ten, were huddled around the fireplace. The grate contained some scanty fuel, and the poor creatures were, in the language of the inspector, "attempting to squeeze the heat out of the bars". The house contained no article of furniture whatsoever, nor was there a morsel of food of any description within the walls … she must have sought subsistence by begging; but, as she never applied to any of the parochial officers for relief, probably from fear of removal, the existence of the family, or their circumstances, were unknown to the authorities of the place. The children stated to the inspector that they had not tasted anything since Saturday morning when the mother distributed amongst them a little bread.[18]

[18] Liverpool Mercury, Jan 30th, 1849, p.8.

CHAPTER TWO

Catholic Irish in Birkenhead

Poverty and Dock Work

In this section I will explain why, in the autumn of 1861, several thousand Birkenhead men were prepared to take up staves and cudgels, with which to attack Irish Catholic residents of the town. The nature of their arrival in the town is a part of the picture. Irish people were escaping famine. They had little or nothing with which to support themselves. They were reduced to begging or seeking help from the Poor Law authorities. However, the Poor Law was designed to punish the poor, it sought to deter people from seeking help. The price of getting help was to be shamed in the eyes of the respectable. Help, when given, was to be given in the workhouse.

In the workhouse families were broken up, husbands from wives, children from parents. They were given distinctive clothing; the clothing was itself a badge of degradation. As late as the 1930s boots provided by the Poor Law authorities marked their wearers out as social pariahs. Such work as was given, or enforced, like stone breaking, was generally pointless and degrading. The Poor Law was intended to make the poor outcasts from the wider society. Charles Booth and Seebohm Rowntree studied poverty in London and York later in the 19th century. They found that only 3% of the population received help from the Poor Law, although 30% were in poverty, in the sense of not having enough to eat.

The Poor Law succeeded in its narrow objective, cutting the amount of money spent on the poor to the minimum. But it did nothing about getting rid of poverty. Rather it made the problem of poverty worse. It created a culture of hatred of the "scroungers" at the bottom of the social ladder. It also ensured the persistence of poverty. If poor people are to escape poverty there needs to be some social, educational, even financial, investment in them. This did not happen in the 19th century; in conditions of austerity it doesn't happen now. The culture of despising the poor persists. So, unsurprisingly, the UK has among the worst levels of child poverty in Europe. Governments, especially Conservative ones, are under no pressure from most of the media, or voters, to make poverty a social priority.

Official attitudes to the poor were harsh, but English authorities did not allow people to starve. This was not the case in Ireland. Many of the Protestant Irish ruling class wanted to be rid of their Catholic tenants. It paid them to turn their land into pasture to raise beef for the British market, to grow grass instead of people. Irish Catholics knew better than to expect charity from their Protestant rulers, even, or perhaps especially, in times of famine. Alexis de Tocqueville, the French philosopher and historian, attended a service in Galway Cathedral in 1835.

> The preacher ended by assuring his audience that the collection was not intended to relieve the wretchedness of Catholics; without doubt all misery ought to concern Christians, but does not scripture say that it is necessary to relieve your own before thinking of strangers? And is not this moral especially applicable, to a small body like that which the Protestants of Galway form, who need to be all united among themselves to enjoy as a living witness of the true religion, without the support of numbers?
>
> I left thinking that charity, so restricted, will hardly destroy the congregation. For in Galway, almost all the Protestants are rich and all the poor, with very

> few exceptions are Catholic.[19]

Karl Marx's friend and benefactor Friedrich Engels had extensive contacts among working class activists, and Trades Unionists, in Manchester. He gave the following description of Irish communities in that city. Attitudes in Liverpool and Birkenhead probably were much the same as those of Engel's informants.

> These Irishmen who migrate for fourpence to England, on the deck of a steamship on which they are often packed like cattle, insinuate themselves everywhere. The worst dwellings are good enough for them; their clothing causes them little trouble, so long as it holds together by a single thread; shoes they know not; their food consists of potatoes and potatoes only; whatever they earn beyond these needs they spend upon drink. What does such a race want with high wages? The worst quarters of all the large towns are inhabited by Irishmen. Whenever a district is distinguished for especial filth and especial ruinousness, the explorer may safely count upon meeting chiefly those Celtic faces which one recognises at the first glance as different from the Saxon physiognomy of the native, and the singing, aspirate brogue which the true Irishman never loses. The majority of the families who live in cellars are almost everywhere of Irish origin. In short, the Irish have, as Dr Kay says, discovered the minimum of the necessities of life, and are now making the English workers acquainted with it. Filth and drunkenness, too, they have brought with them. The lack of cleanliness, which is not so injurious in the country, where population is scattered, and which is the Irishman's second nature, becomes terrifying and gravely dangerous through its concentration here in the great cities. He builds a pigsty against the house

[19] Alexis de Tocqueville's Journey in Ireland, 1835, p. 101

wall as he did at home, and if he is prevented from doing this, he lets the pig sleep in the room with himself. This new and unnatural method of cattle-raising in cities is wholly of Irish origin. The Irishman loves his pig as the Arab his horse, with the difference that he sells it when it is fat enough to kill. Otherwise, he eats and sleeps with it, his children play with it, ride upon it, roll in the dirt with it, as anyone may see a thousand times repeated in all the great towns of England. The filth and comfortlessness that prevail in the houses themselves it is impossible to describe. The Irishman is unaccustomed to the presence of furniture; a heap of straw, a few rags, utterly beyond use as clothing, suffice for this nightly couch. A piece of wood, a broken chair, an old chest for a table, more he needs not; a tea- kettle, a few pots and dishes, equip his kitchen, which is also his sleeping and living room. When he is in want of fuel, everything combustible within his reach, chairs, door- posts, moulding, flooring, finds its way up the chimney. Moreover, why should he need so much room? At home in his mud-cabin there was only one room for all domestic purposes; more than one room his family does not need in England. So the custom of crowding many persons into a single room, now so universal, has been chiefly implanted by the Irish immigration. And, since the poor devil must have one enjoyment, and society has shut him out of all others, he betakes himself to the drinking of spirits. Drink is the only thing which makes the Irishman's life worth having, drink and his cheery carefree temperament; so he revels in drink to the point of the most bestial drunkenness. The southern facile character of the Irishman, his crudity, which places him but little above the savage, his contempt for all humane enjoyment, in which his very crudeness makes him incapable of sharing, his filth and poverty, all favour drunkenness. The temptation is great, he

> cannot resist it, and so when he has money, he gets rid of it down his throat. What else should he do? How can society blame him when it places him in a position in which he almost of necessity becomes a drunkard; when it leaves him to himself, to his savagery?[20]

Engels argues that, in general, poor people were poor not because of their character, as middle-class propaganda maintained, but because they were exploited. Except for Irish poor people, they were poor because of their character.

The people of the Irish slums in Birkenhead also had a reputation for unruliness, sometimes fighting for the fun of it:

> DISTURBANCES BY NAVVIES
>
> On Saturday, some serious affrays took place among the navigators at present employed at the docks, which occasioned considerable alarm to the inhabitants of the locality where they occurred. The first broke out near the docks, on Saturday afternoon, between two parties of "navvies" who arrayed themselves under different leaders. One is known as the Leinster faction, alias Taylor's gang, and the other the Dundalk faction, or McDonald party. Several of the belligerents were severely injured. During the evening of the same day a party of labourers employed at the dock. numbering from 500 to 600 had a faction fight in Watson and Park Streets. The belligerents fought with pokers, sticks, and similar offensive weapons, and we need scarcely say that numerous broken heads and other injuries were the result. The mob was ultimately dispersed by the police.[21]

---

[20] Engels Friedrich The Condition of the Working Class in England, Panther, London, 1969, p. 82

[21] Liverpool Mercury, 20th March, 1849

At other times the violence could be much more organised. The Liverpool Mercury, in February 1857, carried a headline:

> THE STRIKE AT THE BIRKENHEAD DOCK WORKS - THE MILITARY SENT FOR.
>
> The "turnout" of navvies at the Birkenhead docks, which commenced on Monday morning last, still continues, and from present appearances there is no likelihood of the men resuming work, until the demand for an increase of wages from 2s and 8d to 3 shillings per day is conceded. Messrs Thompson the contractors on the other hand, are determined not to employ any of the labourers who have struck, and to supply the places, large bodies of men have been procured from other parts of the country. The "turnouts" however, on each day, have scoured the works, and the new in import navvies, with those who did not strike, have been intimidated and driven from the ground.
>
> On Tuesday morning, the dissatisfied men, to the number of about 300, paraded the township four deep, and halted in the market square where they were addressed by two or three of the number. The speakers emphatically denied that the turnout was one of "Irishmen against Englishman", as had been represented. Their object was solely to obtain an advance of wages from to 2s 9d to 3 shillings a day, which they urged was a very moderate demand, considering the present high prices of provisions and the laborious nature of their employment. A large crowd of spectators was attracted to the square, and to the appeal of the speakers for pecuniary assistance many persons responded.

The magistrates attempted to recruit special constables to protect imported labour, however:

> The bell was rung at one o'clock, when about fifty

> navvies, brought from other contracts, commenced work; but they were not long permitted to proceed with their operations. The 'turnouts' to the number of 300 or 400, who had been concealed behind some of the sandhills in the neighbourhood, suddenly rushed in a body down one of the inclined roads and made a regular onslaught on the works. Their shouts and yells were terrific, and the men who were at work, in a state of alarm, sought safety in otherwise various directions. They were pelted, kicked and their spades were thrown in the dock. The misguided men, having succeeded in their object, then marched off the ground.
>
> Again, the work at the docks was resumed, and was continued for about two hours. In the meantime, the 'turnouts' were not idle. After the assault just alluded to, they proceeded to the North End of Birkenhead, and in Oak Street and other low streets in the locality, enlisted into their army about 200 women and children. They also refreshed themselves with potations of beer and proceeded back to the scene of the campaign, yelling and shouting as they proceeded. The navvies were afterwards conveyed in cabs to Woodside Ferry, it not being safe to remain in Birkenhead during the night. So far, the 'turnouts' were victorious and they left the ground in triumph.[22]

Outbreaks such as described above led many people in England to believe that parts of their towns and cities had been occupied by a foreign people, requiring a different sort of policing. Although Ireland was legally a part of the United Kingdom and had been since the Act of Union in 1800, it would be more accurate to describe it as a British colony. It was certainly policed as a colony. The police were armed, they lived in barracks, not in the community and were discouraged from forming relationships with local communities.

---

[22] Liverpool Mercury, 27th Feb, 1857

British attitudes to the people they colonised were uniformly unfavourable. Colonisers tend to regard the colonised as inferior. This made it easier to justify robbery, exploitation and even enslavement. Alexis de Tocqueville was a French diplomat, writer, and philosopher. He considered England was the best governed country in Europe. He arrived in Ireland in 1835; he soon concluded it was the worst governed. Much of this was to do with the relationship between the anglicised and Protestant ruling class and the native Catholic Irish.

> I have not yet met a man in Ireland, to whatever party he belonged, who did not acknowledge, with more or less bitterness, that the aristocracy had governed the country very badly. The English say it openly, the Orangemen do not deny it, the Catholics shout it at the top of their voices.
>
> I find the language of the aristocracy proves it more than all the rest. All the rich Protestants that I saw in Dublin speak of the Catholic population only with an extraordinary hatred and contempt. They are to all intents savages, incapable of recognising a kindness, fanatics led into every disorder by their priests.[23]

Representations of Irish people in 19th Century cartoons typically showed them as less than human, the kindest showed them as 'less evolved', the cruellest as ape-like.

---

[23] De Tocqueville, op. cit, p. 49

MR. G-O'RILLA, THE YOUNG IRELAND PARTY, EXULTING OVER THE INSULT TO THE BRITISH FLAG. SHOULDN'T HE BE EXTINGUISHED AT ONCE!

Mr G.O'Rilla[24]

[24] John Leech, PUNCH, December 14th, 1861

Racist Representations[25]

In the mid-19th century, black people, Indian people, and the Irish were routinely derided and mocked. In the case of indigenous peoples in the Americas, Australia and New Zealand, there were organised campaigns of extermination. It did not take a great stretch of the imagination for Irish people to believe the same thing was happening to them, especially in the Famine years. Resistance to the colonisation process was ascribed to the "savagery" of the native population. In Ireland such savagery tended to be targeted at expatriate landlords and their agents. Many people in Birkenhead believed they were witnessing Irish "savagery".

[25] H Strickland, Constable, 1899, Ireland from One or Two Neglected Points of View, Wikipedia Commons. File: (*Scientific Racism.* jpg) Accessed 18/09/2020 www.commons.m.wikipedia.org

Battle of the Factions[26]

Rural Irish people had imported the faction fight, which was tolerated in Ireland, into Birkenhead. In July 1835, Alexis de Tocqueville attended the County Waterford Assizes.

> Sixteen cases of murder. All these affairs turned out to be voluntary manslaughter or negligent homicide. but in all these affairs, I believe, a man had been killed. These assizes gave us the very clear impression of the lower classes of this county are very prone to quarrelling and fighting; that nearly every village forms a kind of faction. Factions that began nobody knows when, and continue nobody knows why, without taking on any political significance. When men of these different factions meet each other at a fair, a wedding, or elsewhere, it is rare they do not come to blows for the sole pleasure of the excitement that a fight gives. These quarrels very often end in the death of someone. In general, a

[26] Sean Moraghan, 15/02/2020 (*Days of the Blackthorn*), accessed 18/09/2020, IrishExaminer.com

> man's life here seems to be of very little value.[27]

Men who were involved in what appeared to be a 'fair fight' were often discharged. At the Waterford Assizes in 1835 a man found "Guilty of Manslaughter" received a sentence of 12 months imprisonment. The magistrates of Birkenhead were less tolerant of such disorder.

> DESPERATE FACTION FIGHTS AT BIRKENHEAD
>
> At the Birkenhead police-court, on Monday last, four rough-looking Irishmen, who gave the names of Ward, Sullivan, Kavanagh and Coyle, were brought up charged with rioting and committing an assault upon the police at an early hour of Sunday morning last. It appears that at the North End of the township there are two factions of Irish, denominated the "Connaught men" and the "Dundalk, or north of Ireland men", both of which entertain a strong hatred and animosity towards each other, and the police have frequently considerable difficulty in repressing their feuds. The "Connaught men" inhabit the east end of Oak Street, whilst the west end is occupied by the natives of Dundalk. From the statement of Mr Superintendent McHarg, and the evidence he produced, it seemed that shortly before 12 on Saturday night, the attention of the police was attracted to a disturbance in Oak Street, and on hurrying to the spot they found the two factions arrayed against each other in fierce combat, Park Street, which runs through Oak Street, forming the boundary between the two antagonistic belligerents. Stones and missiles of every size and description were hurled in great profusion by the two mobs, which numbered 300 or 400 persons; but the police, who were pelted with brickbats, succeeded in

[27] De Tocqueville, op. cit, p. 50

> dispersing the parties, and in restoring peace and order to the locality. At half past twelve the police again heard disturbance, and on proceeding to Oak Street they found a large body of the "Connaught men" yelling and shouting like a tribe of Indian savages, the noise being heard at Woodside Ferry. The "Dundalk men" not being turned out, the "Connaught men" commenced an attack upon the police, upon whom they fired a volley of stones and brickbats, besides using other dangerous weapons. Inspector McNeil, and police officers Gunning, Thomson, and Bradshaw were severely struck and abused in the affray. Ultimately, the prisoners who seemed to be the principal actors in the disturbance were taken into custody, and peace was the second time restored. ... Mr Bretherton appeared for the prisoners, and urged that the Mob, lamentable as their proceedings were, had no intention of assaulting the police. The magistrate discharged the prisoner Ward, against whom the evidence was not clear but sent the other three rioters to jail for a month with hard labour.[28]

The Irish population of Birkenhead in the mid-19th century suffered from a number of major disadvantages. They tended to be poor, live in slum areas and were excluded from a range of occupations, particularly skilled ones. Such trades unions as existed were particularly keen to resist competition from Irish workers, along with women and children, who would work for lower wages. Another major disability for most Irish people was religion. They tended to be Catholic and were living in an area where, increasingly, Catholicism was being demonised.

---

[28] Cheshire Observer, 26th August, 1854

CHAPTER THREE

Anti-Catholicism: M'Neile in Liverpool

The Burning of Martyrs[29]

Since the Reformation, British people had been encouraged to think of Catholics, as people under the control of their clergy. Protestant propaganda depicted the suffering of Protestant people in Catholic countries, and in England, when Catholicism was the religion of the land. Such works as Foxe's Book of Martyrs, which was widely read,

---

[29] The Burning of Martyrs; digital image. Posted 2012, accessed 18/09.2020, fineartamerica.com

graphically illustrated the cruelty of Catholic Inquisitions.

The Catholics of Merseyside in general, and Birkenhead in particular, suffered from the zealotry of a group of Protestant clergymen. These most ardent zealots were actually Irish themselves. They had been brought up in the Church of Ireland, the Irish equivalent of the Church of England. Henry VIII had declared himself King of Ireland in 1541 and insisted on extending the Reformation to Ireland. His only problem was that the vast majority of the Irish population did not go along with him. Despite persecution, they remained resolutely Catholic. In fact, the persecution made their resolution stronger.

The Church of Ireland took over all the property that the Catholic Church had in Ireland, churches, cathedrals, monasteries and, crucially, graveyards. This was to become very much of an issue in Birkenhead. Worse, Catholic landowners and tenants were expected to pay for the upkeep of the Church of Ireland, in the form of tithes, those being taxes on landholdings. In the 19th century there were periodic Tithe Wars, systematic and organised refusals to pay tithes. The authorities in Ireland usually reacted with force. Landowners in the rest of Great Britain also resisted paying tithes, but normally peacefully.

The leader of resistance to the payment of tithes and to British rule in Ireland, from the 1820s to the 1840s, was Daniel O'Connell. In 1823 he founded the Catholic Association. He made it the first mass political movement in Europe. Poor people could join by paying a penny a month. At a local level, subscriptions were often collected by Catholic clergy. All of this, and the 'monster meetings' that O'Connell organised in the 1830s and 40s, contributed to a sense among Church of Ireland ministers that they were under siege.

They tended to be virulently anti-Catholic. In the Birkenhead of the 1860s, five out of six Church of England vicars had a background in the Church of Ireland. The once again prosperous town represented a lucrative alternative to impoverished rural Irish livings. Anthony Trollope lived in Ireland for many years. He was very familiar with clergymen of the Church of Ireland. He described them in his work "Clergymen of the Church of England":

THE IRISH BENEFICED CLERGYMAN

The difference between an Irish and an English parson is greater, perhaps, than that which exists between Irishmen and Englishmen of any other special denomination. The normal Irishman is a jolly fellow; but the normal Irish Protestant clergyman is a severe, sombre man, one who speaks of life in sad, subdued tones, one who looks at things around him with a continual remembrance that life is but a span long, that men are but grass of the field, that the sickle is ready and oven heated, and that it is worth no man's while to be comfortable here on earth. He is preaching every moment of his life, preaching in his gait, preaching in every tone of his voice, preaching in every act that he does, preaching in every turn of his eyes. The Irish clergyman does not live in the midst of Protestants with whom he sympathizes but is surrounded by Roman Catholics with whom he cannot sympathize, and against whom he is driven to feel almost a personal enmity, not only by reason of their creed which he sorely hates, but by reason also of the anomalies of his own position which are so hateful to them. Of all men, the Irish beneficed clergyman is the most illiberal, the most bigoted, the most unforgiving, the most sincere, and the most enthusiastic. ...The Irish beneficed clergyman has almost always been educated at Trinity, Dublin, and has there been indoctrinated with those high Protestant principles with which he has before been inoculated. He is, of course, the son of an Irish Protestant gentleman, and has therefore sucked them in with his mother's milk. He goes before his Protestant Bishop and takes his orders with a corps of other young men exactly similarly circumstanced. And thus, he has never had given to him an opportunity of rubbing his own ideas against those of men who have been educated with different proclivities. He has never lived at college either with Roman Catholics, or with Presbyterians, or with

Protestants of a sort different from his sort.[30]

The Irish Beneficent Clergyman[31]

The cartoon above, also taken from Trollope, shows a minister of the Church of Ireland, in a church expropriated from Catholics, preaching

[30] Trollope Anthony, Clergymen of the Church of England, Chapman and Hall, London, 1866, p. 122

[31] Trollope Anthony, Clergymen of the Church of England, Chapman and Hall, London, 1866, p. 123

to a typically sparse rural Protestant congregation. Meanwhile, the Catholics of the parish might be attending an open-air Mass.

The leader of the Protestant Crusade against the Catholic Irish on Merseyside was the Reverend Hugh M'Neile. He made his name in opposing the Liverpool Corporation's provision of schools for poor children. This was for all poor children regardless of their religious affiliation, as was also the case in Ireland. In other towns, education was only available to those who could pay.

According to middle-class opinion at the time, the teaching of religion was the central purpose of education. Given that religion was to be taught in schools there was a question of what religion it was to be.

In Ireland, where the government was keen to instil a sense of discipline in the population, education was a first step in achieving public order. A compromise was reached. It was understood that the Bible, or teachings from it, could be common to both Catholic and Church of Ireland children. Bishops from both churches collaborated in devising a textbook of Biblical extracts which could be used in imparting moral lessons.

But for M'Neile this was an outrage. He believed in the literal truth of the King James version of the Bible - the Authorised Version- any other version, he maintained, was heretical.

The Conservative Party had lost control of Liverpool Council in 1834. It was an incoming Liberal Council which initiated the school experiment. In opposing the schools M'Neile not only attracted support from Tories, he began to exercise control over members of the Tory Party. Thus began a clerical control over Liverpool Conservatives which lasted well into the 20th century. As late as the 1930s a Catholic could not join the Liverpool Conservative Party.

An interested observer of M'Neile was Charles Trevelyan. Trevelyan had introduced a sort of multi- religious education in India for Indian servants of the East India Company. The Company employed Muslims, Sikhs and Hindus. He visited Liverpool in 1840 and wrote an analysis of the Liverpool schools, which he thought could perhaps be a model for a nationwide education system. He observed with alarm M'Neile preaching to a packed congregation in St. Jude's Church:

He made up for lost time by ranting in the most furious manner against the Roman Catholics, drawing the character of their religion as it existed in the dark ages, and maintaining that it had not altered in the least, down to our own time, and in our free Protestant country. "The time was now come," he said, "when everybody must choose between God's side and the devil's. We must fight even unto death. We must lay down our lives rather than submit."

The struggle, which he announced had already begun, was to end only in the entire subjection of either Catholics or Protestants. The missionaries, who have thrown themselves between contending heathen armies, could not rejoice more in the establishment of peace, he then gloried, from the pulpit, in having set Christian against Christian throughout this great nation. I am not alluding here to the general spirit of his sermon, but to express words which he used to that effect. His whole sermon was a savage declaration of war. It was absolutely incendiary, and if the public mind had been in an equally inflammable state, there is no degree of excess to which it might not have led.

In the course of the sermon there was more than one intimation that the Protestants of England were in danger of having the fires of Smithfield lighted again to burn them; but, not being accustomed to this style of preaching, I considered this merely as a rather strong figure of rhetoric. At the end of the sermon, however, I was shocked and confounded by hearing God solemnly called to witness to similar ridiculous misrepresentations. The preacher besought the Almighty, with extraordinary emphasis, that the Protestant population of England might not be deprived of the use of their bibles and pulpits. Could Loyala himself go beyond this? I could not refrain from taking a survey of the faces of the persons

> sitting in the pews behind me, after two or three of the grossest and most ridiculous parts of the sermon, expecting to see them bursting with laughter or indignation; but, with the exception of two or three young men, who appeared to have been drawn thither by curiosity, and who had, certainly, a broad smile playing on their countenances, the rest of the congregation were hanging on the lips of the preacher, and drinking in, with the most profound reverence, every word that fell from him.
>
> What is there wanting, except the power of ordering his victims to the stake, to complete the resemblance between the preacher before us, and a Popish Vicar Apostolic of the dark ages? There was the same unbounded reliance on the mental and moral prostration of his flock; there was the same tyrannous hate of those who differed from him in opinion; there was the same gross misrepresentation of the principles and practice of his opponent.
>
> The Preacher asserted that Roman Catholicism is incompatible with free principles of government, forgetting, or not knowing, that the Irish, the Poles, the Belgians, the French, the Spaniards, the Portuguese, the inhabitants of the different states of South America, the Piedmontese, the Lombards, the Neapolitans, and even the inhabitants of the Papal states, have achieved for themselves constitutional government, Or have made great sacrifices to obtain it, to say nothing of the old Roman Catholic cantons of Switzerland, which are the nucleus of Swiss liberty, and the most popular governments in the world.[32]

Frightening people was, and still is, a branch of public entertainment. Now we have horror in film and books and on TV. In the 1860s resources were somewhat more limited. The horror sermon could be

---

[32] Trevelyan, op. cit, p. 33

both an entertainment and the road to advancement in the Church. Anthony Trollope certainly perceived this. In his book 'The Clergymen of the Church of England' he had a chapter 'The Town Incumbent' in which he outlined the pressures on a clergyman to achieve the sort of notoriety that M'Neile had attained:

> For him there must always be poverty and hard work, or - that worst of all poverty which has to hide itself under a black coat, and work which is not only ceaseless, but too often thankless and apparently without adequate results! This must be his lot in life, he tells himself, - unless he can preach himself into a reputation. If he can do that, if he can be a McNeal (sic) or an English Ward Beecher, then, indeed, there will be a career open to him. This after all is what men want, town incumbents as well as others; and so the town incumbent sets himself to work to make a reputation for himself by pulpit eloquence. As he walks along the dull new street of his district, he fills himself with this ambition and declares to himself that he will be great as a preacher. He will fill his seats, and draw men to him, - or if not men, at least women. He will denounce sins with a loud voice and eager accents, and he will denounce not only sins, but heresies also, and lax doctrines. By denouncing simply sin, few clerical aspirants have become noted by their neighbours, but the man who will denounce his neighbours' opinions as well as his sins will become famous. And so the town incumbent settles himself to his desk and goes to work. ... Given the church to fill, and the incumbency to be made valuable by filling it, and it is simply human nature that an energetic man shall endeavour to fill his church and make his profession valuable. He cannot fill his church by visiting the poor. He cannot earn for himself even the decent position in the district in which he lives by careful performance of ordinary clerical duties. If he simply reads the services and

> officiates at the Communion table and preaches drowsy sermons, he will starve on some two hundred pounds a year and never get his head above water, either as regards money or reputation. Of course, he will do his best for himself, and of course he will teach himself to believe that in doing so he is doing the best for the cause which he really loves in his heart. He is not a bad man or a hypocrite, because he denounces heresies and lax doctrines in a loud voice, instead of endeavouring to teach his people simply that they should not lie or get drunk, or steal. He is probably a very good man; but he is a good man who would like to have one thousand pounds a year and the name, instead of two hundred pounds a year and no name at all.[33]

Daniel O'Connell visited Liverpool in August 1842 and spoke at the opening of a Catholic church in the city. He addressed the problems that M'Neile was causing for Catholics and denounced both him and his conservative allies with withering scorn.

> He did not know any place where he should more like to address words of sarcasm and scorn to the bigots ... there was no spot in which he would more delight to do all this than in their town of Liverpool. (Cheers.) Would they be so good as to tell him whether there was a more bigoted town in the British empire? Because if there was, he would go and look for it. (Much laughter and cheering.) For his own part, he was convinced that there was more practical bigotry in Liverpool than in any ten towns of Great Britain. (Laughter and cheers.) Why they encouraged it. It was in their politics, - for bad politics made bigots; it was in the Corporation, which was unchristian in its proceedings, because the majority were bigots; it was in their return of members of

[33] Trollope, op. cit, p33

> Parliament.
>
> If they sent another batch of bigots, they would be worse than the M'Neiles, who were worse than the devil. (Much laughter). He liked to laugh at them; but what an excellent trade lying was to the fellow. His very uncharitableness was paid for by the yard; his falsehoods and calumnies were paid for by the pound weight, and such a traffic in bigotry, falsehood, and calumny was never established in any town as that established in the trading town of Liverpool. (Cheers.) It was melancholy to think that a man should desecrate the temple of the God of charity by the utterance of everything bigoted, foul, and false; that he should scorn the path of truth; that he should abandon every portion of that benevolence with Providence intended as the bond of union between man and man, and between that being and Himself; that charity should be outraged, and bigotry assuming its place should supersede it in the high places, in the streets, and in the pulpit, and that M'Neile should be followed and courted because he was the deuce's own lump of a liar. (Loud laughter.)[34]

For all the disdain shown to M'Neile by Trevelyan and O'Connell and other liberal commentators, there is no doubting the effectiveness of his campaign. An incoming Conservative administration in 1842 pronounced that the Authorised Version would be used in Corporation schools. Most Catholic pupils were withdrawn. This delayed the introduction of a national system of education for at least 30 years.

In Liverpool itself, Trevelyan noted the poisoning of relationships between different Christian sects and the antagonism being directed to the Corporation pupils:

> Unhappily, however, ... harmony is confined to the

[34] Liverpool Mercury, 12th Aug, 1842

> interior of the school. The moment the Masters and boys leave the school, they become liable to insult and outrage. They are constantly hooted at, and taunted with being papists, and the children have often been cruelly beaten. The principal agents in this persecution of the boys belonging to the neighbouring opposition schools. The sticks and stones used by them in making their assaults have been taken out of their hands; and it became necessary to station an extra policeman to protect the boys belonging to the Corporation schools from their violence ... when the incendiary speeches and sermons constantly delivered by persons whose talent and station in the church give them great power over the ignorant, heady multitude, are considered, the wonder will be that far greater outrages than these are not committed against these schools, and whatever else is connected with the concession of equal civil privileges to Roman Catholics. The perfect harmony which prevails inside the corporation schools, and the deadly hatred and open violence which prevail outside, are an awful reproof to those ministers of discord who openly glory from the pulpit in having set one- half the country against the other half.[35]

M'Neile, in exploiting social hatred, was an early example of a populist politician, comparable to the early Ian Paisley, Donald Trump or Boris Johnson. Populist politicians, like M'Neile, play on people's fears. They focus hatred on outsiders. He remained a dominant figure in Liverpool politics until the 1860s. A statue to him was commissioned in 1872. It still stands in St. George's Hall. The installation had to be done secretly and at dead of night, so fearful were the authorities of Catholic reprisals.

---

[35] Trevelyan, op. cit, p33

Statue of M'Neile[36]

The Liverpool Mail in 1848 had a report on a religious meeting in which M' Neile and his supporters were involved:

> Dr M'Neile's oratorical displays are also attended usually by his special bodyguards, impressively known as the 'Protestant Boys' - many of them much more familiar with brickbats and bludgeons than with Bible and prayer book. His militant worthies swarm in every meeting, and are ready to clamour down, ay, or to knock down, any English clergyman or English gentleman who, in the legitimate exercise

[36] M'Neile in St Georges Hall

of his right of membership in this or that society, has the temerity openly to differ, however reasonably, however temperately, from the narrow and intolerant dogmatizing of their idol.

Then again Liverpool has become such a colony of immigrant Irish clergy, that an independent English clergyman has no chance of a fair hearing. With one or two honourable exceptions on both sides of the Mersey, the main body of Irish clergymen in this town and neighbourhood are Dr M' Neile's subservient fuglemen and clamorous claqueurs at these public performances. He thinks for them. They puppet-like do his bidding. They call his bitter, sweet; his wilfulness and wrongheadedness, firmness; his aspiring vanity, inspired zeal.

They hold it almost semi-blasphemy for any person to question the conclusions or the conduct of one to whose coattails they cling, for the reflex of his mob popularity. The spirit of Irish "faction" in them is so strong and so blinds them whatever understanding they possess, that they perpetrate incredible outrages on the understanding of Englishmen.

... What next? An intolerant Irish Inquisition, less endurable than the Spanish, would shortly be set up in Liverpool, and Englishmen, clergy and laity alike, be subjected to its petty annoyances, if colonised Irish priests are thus shamelessly to pervert truth and justice to serve their own selfish ends and to combine to "put down" the native English.[37]

---

[37] Liverpool Mail, 21st October, 1848

Richard Smith[38]

There had been sectarian violence in Liverpool before M'Neile arrived in 1834, but it grew under his guidance. He attracted Protestant working class Liverpudlians, afraid of Irish competition for work and wages. He also attracted other Church of Ireland bigots, such as the Rev. Dr Baylee. The Reverend Joseph Baylee arrived in England in 1838, Baylee and M'Neile worked together to minister to various Protestant Operative Associations. These were key working-class bodies bent on excluding Catholics from skilled trades and from political office, as well as forming the nucleus of anti-Catholic mobs throughout the 1840s and 1850s.

---

[38] The Church Magazine, Vol.1, No.7, (July 1839), facing page 193.

With his Billy Boy, bully boy tactics, his beliefs in racial superiority, his advocacy of violence against non- believers and his desire for the exclusion of the inferior from any political life, M'Neile could reasonably be described as a protofascist. He established a tradition which was still alive in the 1930s. Barbara Whittingham-Jones, then herself a Conservative Party member, described what she witnessed when she attended a meeting of the Liverpool Working Men's Conservative Association in 1936. For members of the WMCA, despite the dangers to the British Empire of expansionism from Hitler's Germany, Mussolini's Italy and Japan in the Far East, the real danger was Irish republicanism and Catholicism.

> The Chairman (or Chairwoman) opens the meeting by requiring members who have been guilty of 'consorting' with Catholics to confess their delinquencies and upon doing so they then receive a warning. Catholics who have strayed in by chance are requested to leave the room.
>
> Even questions have to be preceded by the formula 'by my Protestant faith and conservative principles...', with hand raised in the Hitler salute. Such is the democratic character of this sectarian, class ridden Caucus, that no Roman Catholic working man can join the Conservative Party in Liverpool for the minimum annual subscription of one shilling or frequent the working men's Conservative clubs. It is hardly surprising that the majority of the poorer members of the Roman church vote for the Socialist party.[39]

Both M'Neile and Baylee were products of Trinity College Dublin. Trinity College in the early 19th century was very much a machine for churning out Evangelicals to staff the Church of Ireland. It was divorced from and hostile to the Catholic population of the country. De Tocqueville spent the day of July 9th, 1835, visiting first the Dublin

[39] Whittingham-Jones Barbara, The Pedigree of Liverpool politics. White, Orange and Green, Liverpool, 1936

Poorhouse and then Trinity College.

A vast edifice sustained by voluntary gifts. 1,800 to 2,000 are received there during the day; they receive food, lodging, and when they are capable of it, work. They go to sleep where they can.

The sight inside. The most hideous and disgusting aspect of destitution. A very long room full of women and children whose infirmity or age prevent them from working. On the floor the paupers are lying down pell-mell like pigs in the mud of the stye. One has difficulty not to step on a half-naked body.

In the left wing, in a smaller room, they are seated on wooden benches, all turned in the same direction, crowded together as in the pit of a theatre. They do not talk at all, all they do not move, look at nothing, they do not appear to be thinking. They neither expect, fear, nor hope for anything from life. I am mistaken, they're waiting for dinner, which is due in three hours. It is the only pleasure that is left to them, after which they will have nothing more than to die.

Further on, are those who are able to work. They are seated on the damp earth. They have small mallets in their hands and are breaking stones. At the end of the day they receive a penny... They are the lucky ones.

On leaving there we came upon a small covered wheelbarrow pushed by two paupers. This wheelbarrow goes to the door of the houses of the rich; into it is thrown the remains of the meals, and this debris is brought to the Poorhouse to make soup.

From the Poorhouse they took us to the university, an immense and magnificent garden kept up like that of a nobleman. A palace of granite, a superb church, a wonderful library. Lackeys in livery, 24 Fellows, 70 scholars. enormous revenues. Men of all religions are educated there. But only members of the Church of England can administer the establishment and

> receive its revenues.
>
> This university was founded by Elizabeth with the estates confiscated from Catholics, the fathers of those whom we had just seen wallowing in the mud at the poorhouse. This establishment contains 1,500 students. Very few belong to rich Irish families. Not only do the Irish nobility live abroad; not only do they spend abroad the money it (Ireland) produces, but they rear their children in England, for fear undoubtedly that the vague instinct of patriotism and fond memories might bind them one day to Ireland.
>
> If you wish to know what the spirit of conquest, religious hatred, combined with all the abuses of aristocracy but none of its advantages, can produce, come to Ireland.[40]

This was the sort of society that M'Neile wished to see reproduced in Liverpool. M'Neile was firmly convinced that God took an active part in human history. For all his religiosity he could not be considered a kind or forgiving man. The Liverpool Mercury in November 1849, commented on a speech given by M'Neile to the Church Missionary Society. Even the editor of the Mercury was incredulous at what he got away with saying, and that he was even applauded. The famine was an act of God, for which they, as missionaries to Ireland, should be thankful. There are not many Christian pastors prepared to see the good side of a famine, but it was only Catholics that were dying.

> However, as a matter of mere speculative curiosity, our readers may be interested to see a point beyond which the force of bigotry can no further go. The fiendish shout of exultation which hailed the Rev. Mr M'Neile's allusion to the Irish millions thinned by famine, was indeed a sincere exchange for the mask of hypocritical kindness which such a wicked enterprise had assumed. We wonder that any system of church discipline should exist, not containing a

---

[40] De Tocqueville, op. cit, pp. 24-26.

> provision for restraining persons in the position of clergymen from discrediting so outrageously the common name of Christianity, as that divine does in the following passage:
>
> "How wonderful is the providence of God. In the days of old a proud ruler of Israel commenced a numbering of their people. The answer of Divine Providence was to thin their numbers. Retribution fell, not upon the head of the offender, but upon 70,000 who had in that matter not offended. The leaders of Romanism in Ireland boasted of their millions; they terrified England with their millions, they shouted in parliament their millions; their great leader who is gone to his account exaggerated their millions. The pressure from without became stronger and stronger, and God has thinned the ranks of these millions." (Loud cheers.)[41]

To put this in context, in 1841, a census year, the population of England and Wales was about 16 million, that of Ireland was 8 million. Irish people, if they were united, as O'Connell was succeeding in doing, could be construed as a considerable force in the United Kingdom. By 1861 the population of England and Wales was over 19 million, that of Ireland was 4 1/2 million. Ireland was becoming a small offshore problem.

Anti-Catholicism became an important factor in Liverpool politics from the 1830s. At the same time, anti-Irish and anti-Catholic sentiment was growing in North America, where those Irish who could afford it went. The movements fed off each other. The Cork Examiner noted the resemblance:

> NATIVE AMERICAN PHILOSOPHY
>
> The Orangemen of Ireland and the Native American are political twins. The one would govern Ireland, and the other America, for themselves alone. Then they are both generous of words and

[41] Cork Examiner, 28th November, 1849

> professions of kindness. The Bible is never out of their mouths, but never in their heart, but all the time they are tyrants and blasphemers of Christian truth, and shedders of innocent blood.
>
> Through the whole maze of words and mysticism of ideas which run through this American declaration, we can only discover that it is mainly aimed at Irish Catholic immigrants ... instead of thanking the gods for this influx of human Labour and capital - for turning their forests into harvest field-pushing civilization and cities into the heart of her untrodden prairies - rendering the bosoms of her lakes and rivers perpetually populous - for manning her fleets and armies, and adding to her literature and science - here is young America, instead of advancing with the march of mind and the spirit of the times, wrapping herself up in a mantle of intolerance, and propounding Dogma which would be a disgrace to the most despotic old state in Europe.[42]

The birth of the Know Nothing party, the Native American political party, which fought elections in the 1840s and 50s, came with the burning down of a Catholic convent at Charlestown, near Boston, in 1834. There had been a background of rumours in the town that women and girls were being held in the convent against their will.

> Anti-Catholicism has always been the pornography of the Puritan. Whereas the anti- Masons had envisaged drinking bouts and had entertained themselves with sadomasochistic fantasies about the actual enforcement of grizzly Masonic oaths, the anti-Catholics invented an immense lore about libertine priests, the confessional as an opportunity for seduction, licentious convents and monasteries. Probably the most widely read contemporary book in

---

[42] Cork Examiner, Sep 8th, 1845

> the United States before Uncle Tom's Cabin was a work supposedly written by one Mariah Monk, entitled Awful Disclosures, which appeared in 1836. The author, who purported to have escaped the Hotel Dieu Nunnery in Montreal after five years there as a novice and nun, reported her convent life in elaborate and circumstantial detail. She reported having been told by the Mother Superior that she must "obey the priests in all things"; to her "utter astonishment and horror", she soon found out what the nature of such obedience was. Infants born of convent liaisons were baptised and then killed, she said, so that they might ascend at once to Heaven. Her book, hotly attacked and defended, continued to be read and believed even after her mother gave testimony that Maria had been somewhat addled ever since childhood after she had rammed a pencil into her head. Maria died in prison in 1849, after having been arrested in a brothel as a pickpocket.[43]

The Conservative and anti-Catholic newspapers of Liverpool went to town on stories of Mariah Monk as did M'Neile. He was not above adding a touch of salaciousness to his sermons and addresses. Some newspapers printed whole chapters from the 'Awful Disclosures'. The following is an edited extract from the Liverpool Standard:

> POPERY IN AMERICA
>
> We take the following most extraordinary narrative from an American paper, the Albany Transcript, which appears to borrow it from the New York Journal of Commerce. The details here given are almost beyond the bounds of credibility, but we are assured that every word is true! Can we wonder, then, at the crimes and demoralisation of the Roman Catholics of Ireland, when under the sanction of their

[43] Hofstadter, Richard (November 1962), 'The Paranoid style in American Politics', Harper's Magazine, retrieved October 5th, 2020

religion we see profligacy and horrid enormities?

AWFUL DISCLOSURES, by Maria Monk

Which, if a true narrative, and there is strong internal evidence of it being so, throws "Six Months in a Convent" very far into the shade. It purports to be a statement by Miss Monk, "of her suffering during a residence of five years as a novice, and two years as a black nun, in the Hotel Dieu Nunnery, at Montreal." This woman, it seems, is, or has recently been, an inmate of the New York Almshouse, having taken refuge there after her escape from the nunnery, and ere long giving birth to a child! She represented herself and all the other nuns in that Convent to have been continually subject to the approaches of the priests, whose licentiousness exceeded all sounds. She details many instances of the murder of the offspring of the nuns in the convent, some of which he witnessed with her own eyes. In some instances, nuns themselves were murdered. The following is her account of a scene of this description:

In reply to some of the questions put to her she was silent; to others I heard her voice reply that she did not repent of words she had uttered, though it had been reported by some of the nuns who had heard them, that she still wished to escape from the convent; and that she had firmly resolved to resist every attempt to compel her to the commission of crimes which she detested. She added that she would rather die than cause the murder of harmless babes.

"That is enough, finish her!" said the bishop. Two nuns instantly fell upon the young woman, and in obedience to directions given by the superior, prepared to execute her sentence.

She seized a gag, forced it into the mouth of the poor nun, and when it was fixed between her extended jaws so as to keep them open at the greatest distance, took hold of the strap fastened at each end of the stick, trussed them behind the helpless head of

> the victim, and drew them tight through the loop prepared as a fastening.
>
> … On the bed, the prisoner was laid with her face upward and then bound with cords so that she could not move. In an instant, another bed was thrown upon her. One of the priests, named Bonin, sprang like a fury first upon it, and stamped upon it with all his force. He was speedily followed by the nuns, until there were as many upon the bed as could find room, and did what they could, not only to smother her, but to bruise her. Some stood up and jumped upon the poor girl with their feet, some with their knees, and others, in different ways, seemed to seek how they might just beat the breath out of her body, and mangle it, without coming in direct contact with it, or seeing the effect of the violence. During this time, my feelings were almost too strong to be endured, I felt stupefied, and scarcely was conscious of what I did. Still, fear for myself remained in a sufficient degree to induce me to some exertion, and I attempted to talk to those who stood next, partly that I might have an excuse for turning away from the dreadful scene.[44]

Such accounts of torture, murder and sexual misbehaviour proved very titillating to the ultra- Protestants of Liverpool. M'Neile was still referencing them nearly 20 years later in an address at Liverpool's Royal Amphitheatre:

> Moreover, then, she was listening too in her very dreams, and she pulled out the sympathies of her heart, perhaps unconsciously; these discoveries were reported again to the spiritual mother of the convent, and once retailed to the director or confessor; and who could tell what was the system of ordeal then pursued, or the fearful crushing down of all that was dear, and human, and social, in the soul of the poor

[44] Liverpool Standard, 4th March, 1836

nun?

... And then let him remind them that if the poor nun once became the victim of the mother of the convent, she also became the victim of the confessor of the convent. Oh, what a petty tyrant was the priest within the walls of the convent! There no man could interfere to check his authority - there no one could bring a counter acting influence to his intrigue and despotism. If they asked him why a priest should not live in a nunnery, he would answer, if for nothing else, because of the power they were able to exercise there. (Hear, Hear.) If they asked him what were the principles of popery, he would say ambition for power; and if they asked why that was, he would reply because such a failing was the chief failing of the universal world. Pride and ambition, the greatest sins of mankind, had cast down our first parents from paradise; and it was this priest's love of power that actuated popery to build up that stupendous structure, the most marvellous the world ever witnessed, the mystery of iniquity.

... Then they could conceive how the poor nuns fell down before this man - the only man that ever came amongst them except the bishop now and then, perhaps (laughter and cheers) - for if they did hear a little of gossip or scandal, or what was going on in the forbidden world, they had to depend for it on the priest; he was the newspaper as he was the prayer book; there was no other earthly being to whom they could confide their secrets and sorrows; and if this priest be a fascinating and insinuating man, oh, what, indeed, must be the power he exercised over those poor women. (Laughter.) This was a power which he knew to be all his own; it was a fearful autocracy, for he reigned alone, and no one could dispute his power or interfere with his authority; and he might well truthfully say with Alexander Selkirk, he was lord of all he surveyed. (Hear.) There was, let them bear in

> mind - in these dismal abodes, no brother to take an oppressed sister's part; no father to step between the ghostly father and the poor oppressed nun: who then could tell what scenes might occur within these prison walls? (Hear, Hear.) He did not mean to speak of their knowledge of these dreadful atrocities in their own country, but they had come to the knowledge of the world indisputable evidence of disclosures of scenes in nunneries elsewhere which were calculated to make hell turn pale; they had heard of pits into which babes were cast till they were almost filled up with bones; and ought they then to say they had no right to know what went on within the walls of nunneries in this land? ("Hear, hear" and cries of "We will".) It was the duty of every man to be the defender of the weak, the vindicator of the oppressed. ("Hear, hear" and applause.) there were a thousand chords with an English heart that still operated in the heart sympathies being enlisted in their behalf. (Cheers.)[45]

So, according to M'Neile and his associates, the chief problem with clerics of the Catholic Church was their lust for power. At the level of the individual priest, it was power over those around them, especially women. At an institutional level it was power over whole nations, even the British Empire.

[45] Liverpool Mercury, April 30th, 1852

THE KIDNAPPER.—A CASE FOR THE POLICE.

The Kidnapper[46]

[46] John Leech, Punch, March 29th, 1852, p. 129

CHAPTER FOUR

Baylee in Birkenhead

Baylee came to Birkenhead in 1841 as the Vicar of the newly built Holy Trinity Church in Price Street. By 1862 he had succeeded in disciplining the new MP for Birkenhead, John Laird, and the Birkenhead Conservative Party into becoming a sectarian anti-Catholic force. He also succeeded in gaining the town a reputation for anti-Catholic violence, a reputation it shared with M'Neile's Liverpool. He was instrumental in founding St Aidan's Theological College in Birkenhead and acted as its principal for many years. His objective was to widen the intake of recruits for the ministry of the Church of England. He encouraged working class men to become Bible Readers and even clergymen. He was also a prolific author. It is a shame that his works are now unreadable. His assumptions are fantastical to the modern mind. They promoted his beliefs in the literal truth of the Bible. He attempted to apply the prophecies of the Book of Revelations to current political and social issues, for example, describing the Irish famine as a foreshadowing of the Apocalypse. He attacked Science, especially Geology, Darwinism, Catholicism and Unitarianism. Baylee was seldom guilty of showing a Christian forbearance to his opponents.

The Catholics of Birkenhead were told what they might expect from him. Baylee had played a leading role in The Achill Island colony. The leaders of the Church of Ireland, led by M'Neile's father-in-law, the Archbishop of Dublin, had mounted a Protestant Crusade to convert Catholics to the Church of Ireland, starting in the

1820s. However, such converts as were made often found themselves ostracised, even attacked, by their Catholic neighbours. In those circumstances, some members of the Church of Ireland decided that converts should be gathered in a model settlement where pressure from Catholic neighbours could be resisted. On Achill, however the situation was reversed, the pressure came from the converts and their ministers on the original inhabitants of the island. In a letter to the Catholics of Birkenhead, the Catholic Archbishop of Tuam pointed out how Baylee had behaved on Achill Island.

Woodcut of Achill Colony[47]

MEETING OF THE CATHOLICS OF BIRKENHEAD.

On Monday evening last a meeting of the Catholics of Birkenhead was held at the school room attached to the chapel of that town, for the purpose of establishing a branch of the Catholic Institute of Great Britain. The meeting was attended by all the leading Catholics of that neighbourhood, assisted by several gentlemen from Liverpool. The room was very much crowded, and the audience took great interest in the proceedings.

---

[47] John Barrow 'A Tour Round Ireland Through the Sea Coast Counties, in the Autumn of 1835', Irish Times; updated Sep 18th 2018, accessed Sep 23rd 2020

The Reverend Doctor Butler, who was most warmly received in coming forward to second the fourth resolution, commenced by complementing, in flattering terms, the gentlemen who were appointed members of the committee. He then dwelt forcibly upon the great duty of Catholics to enlighten all who are ignorant of, or hostile to the Catholic religion. He appealed to their own knowledge of the incessant activity of a local clergyman of the establishment, who made use of every means to poison the minds of well-meaning Protestants by gross misstatements and distorted representations of Catholic principles. He happily alluded to the persecutions said to have been suffered by the gentleman in Ireland, and in allusion to them read the following excellent letter from Dr M'Hale.

'St. Jarlath, Tuam, May 17th, 1841.

Rev. Dear Sir, - I have been favoured with your kind letter, enclosing a printed document bearing the signature of Joseph Baylee. This gentleman, who, I suppose, alludes to me as the popish archbishop, so takes care to hide the extraordinary history of his persecutions and sufferings in indistinct generalities as must convince every intelligent reader that he has unsparingly drawn upon his own imagination. It is scarcely to be expected that I would so trespass on your time as to be giving a detailed contradiction to a series of such romantic, and I trust, even to an English Protestant audience, such harmless inventions. Suffice it to say that if Mr Baylee be one of the self-sent missionaries that engaged in the frantic undertaking of seducing the natives of Achill or Clare Ireland from out of the pale of the Catholic Church, he, no doubt, must have shared in the dignified reproofs and spiritual denunciations pointed by the inspired writers against those who are guilty of leading souls from the path of truth and virtue. If against repeated admonitions he was found forcing himself into the cottages of the faithful and filling their ears with the most blasphemous words regarding the Blessed Eucharist, as well as calumnies on their revered pastors. I should not be surprised if he was reminded that the poor people of Achill had their rights as well as those of England; that their cabins, however wretched, were as much their rightful castles as the baronial palace was of its proud occupants, and it that is was as lawful for the one to repel the insidious and forcible aggressors of their faith as for the other to repel the invader of his property. Beyond the exercise of this just vigilance on the part of the pastors, and self-defence on the part of the people, the supposed persecutions against this rev. missionary were not carried. If he be one of those who obtruded himself insolently among the people in Clare Island during the administration of the sacrament of confirmation, when it would appear to be the object to provoke a breach of the peace, he ought to recollect with gratitude the seasonable interposition of the clergy in protecting those ministers of delusion. Were it not for the lessons of peace and charity that we constantly inculcate, exhorting the people not to return evil for evil, but overcome evil with good, these deceivers of the English might have an opportunity of exhibiting to the auditory the evidence of their stripes, rather than be amusing them with the legends of the romantic descent of a steep cliff of 400 feet - an indecent, and like the rest of his letter, a profane parody on the labours and persecutions of the great apostle.

From the excellent specimens laid before the public of your exposition of the Catholic faith, it is not likely that this reverend gentleman will be more successful in the neighbourhood of Liverpool than he has been in Connaught. For your vindication of Saint Bernard, you are entitled to the gratitude of the Protestants, whom you rescued from such gross delusion. The

> controversialists will, I trust, be more cautious in abusing the history of past times. Wishing you every success in your present laudable efforts in exposing the misrepresentations of our venerated creed, I have the honour to be, Rev. Dear Sir.
> Your faithful servant,
> John, archbishop of Tuam'.[48]

It should be noted here that the Rev. Dr Butler, who in the 1830s and early 1840s was the leading Catholic critic of both M'Neile and Baylee, by 1848 had become Baylee's ally. In fact, he played a leading part in the anti-Catholic provocation which came to be known as the Garibaldi riots.

In his early life Baylee developed a set of practices to which he remained true his entire career: telling lies about the doctrines of other Christian sects, confronting the clerics of other sects and the posting of placards. He attracted publicity in Dublin for his anti-Unitarian dirty tricks. The Unitarians were, and are, a Christian sect who deny that God exists as a Trinity, but rather in the form of one God. This, no doubt, is why Baylee's church was called Holy Trinity. What follows was taken from the Dublin Evening Post of July 1838:

> It seems that in the course of last week some placards were published setting forth, in very offensive terms, that the doctrine of the Trinity was to be impugned at the Unitarian Chapel Eustace Street, on Wednesday last. The presence of the orthodox being at the same time invited. The consequence was the gathering of a mob at the place of worship, but it seems there was not the remotest intention of raising any polemical question whatsoever ... out of this affair the following correspondence arose.[49]

From this opening paragraph there followed a correspondence between Baylee and one of the Unitarian ministers involved, James

[48] Freeman's Journal, 30th Sep, 1841

[49] Dublin Evening Post, 12th July, 1838

Armstrong. His comments on Baylee's conduct are enlightening:

> I presume you were one of the gentlemen who, attended by a multitude of persons evidently in a state of great excitement, assembled ... on Wednesday last. I perfectly recollect the conversation I had with those gentlemen - I perfectly recollect declaring my peremptory disavowal of the placard put into my hands, and which I then saw for the first time - I perfectly recollect, too, when they mentioned their readiness to defend the peculiar views in a viva voce discussion, that I absolutely decline such a measure, not only then, but at all times. It appears to me, that clerical adventurers have adopted this as a mode of raising themselves from obscurity, after having by the declamatory harangues flattered the prejudice of the church and her partisans and they sometimes obtain well filled purses or rich benefits as the reward of the championship in the ecclesiastical crusade.[50]

The living at Holy Trinity Church was indeed a well filled purse, and a well-known troublemaker officiated over it.

50 Ibid

Holy Trinity Church[51]

Baylee's reputation among Birkenhead Catholics was certainly not enhanced by the events of July 12th, 1843. In 1843 the Liverpool Mercury reprinted a story which had appeared earlier in the Liverpool Standard, a Tory newspaper and supportive of the Orange Order:

[51] Holy Trinity Church, Price Street, Birkenhead. From wirralmemories.co.uk, accessed 22.07.22

PROCESSION OF ORANGE LODGES AT BIRKENHEAD

Wednesday last being the anniversary of the "Battle of the Boyne" two of the Liverpool lodges connected with this loyal and powerful body proceeded by the Woodside steamers to the Wheat Sheaf, North Birkenhead, where they were joined by several friends, and thence walked in procession, headed by band of music, to Trinity Church, where an excellent and truly appropriate sermon was preached by the Rev J. Baylee, which was listened to with the most marked attention. After service they again formed, and proceeded through Birkenhead to Bebington, and back by Hamilton Square to Woodside, when those at once connected with North Birkenhead Lodge, preceded by the band, filed off to the Lodge House; a most excellent and substantial dinner was served up. The members of the other lodges assembled to witness the return. Each member wore the favours of the society, and, as well as other ornaments illustrative of the glorious achievements in the day they commemorated. It is worthy of remark, that, though the procession was assailed more than once by the slanderous tongues of disaffected persons, who appeared greatly annoyed by its respectability and imposing effect, not one member evinced the slightest disposition to a breach of the peace, which it was evidently the purpose of their invidious opponents to provoke.

If the Cheshire Magistrates do their duty, they will prevent these *loyal* gentry from having any more such exhibitions at Birkenhead. These Orange lodges are illegal bodies, being bound together by secret oaths, signs and passwords, and the nature of their *loyalty* maybe guessed from the fact that, in 1834, the leaders were proved to have been tampering with the army, with the supposed view of altering the succession to the throne.[52]

The Unlawful Oaths Act, which applied only in Ireland, had in effect made it illegal to join the Orange Order. The plot that the Mercury refers to, surrounded the figure of Ernest Augustus, the fifth son of George III. Ernest Augustus was a die-hard anti-Catholic Tory, an opponent of Catholic Emancipation and Imperial Grand Master of the Orange Order. As a general in the British Army, he had advocated the establishment of Orange Lodges in the army. The Orange Order was accused of plotting to place him on the throne on the death of William IV. The king took action, under Parliamentary pressure, and Ernest Augustus, Duke of Cumberland and later King of Hanover, was forced to disband the Orange Lodges.

Birkenhead's first, but by no means last Orange march, was held in arrangement with Baylee, perhaps at his invitation. Baylee brought his penchant for placarding to Birkenhead. It should be noted that his placards were often printed on orange paper or card, to make more obvious, if it were possible, his association with the Orange Order. Orange placards were illegal in Ireland because of their association with the Orange Order and with civil unrest. One example, in 1849, was a placard posted all over Birkenhead; it read:

> THE RIVAL CATHOLICS
>
> The Reverend Joseph Baylee who caught and converted a Roman Catholic priest, the Rev Thomas Butler the other day, seems to have been dreadfully annoyed that a convert the other way, late curate to the Reverend Dr Hook, of Leeds, should be announced to preach at St Werburgh's Chapel, and, most especially, that said Chapel should be called "Catholic", the Rev. Joseph claiming the monopoly of that title for himself, and those who think with him. He has, therefore, flared up against it in a placard, which has been pasted all over Birkenhead, and which commences as follows:
>
> 'CATHOLIC CHURCH

[52] Liverpool Mercury, 19th July, 1843

An announcement having been made by Public Placard, that the late Protestant curate of Dr Hook of Leeds,' is to preach at 'the Catholic church of St Werburgh's'. I am reluctantly compelled to make this public protest, against an assumption which has no real foundation. The building referred is only A ROMANIST PLACE OF WORSHIP and has no claim to be a Catholic Church. Its priests have no authority in this Parish; and they do not teach the truth of God as set forth in his Holy Word, and in the teaching of the ancient Catholic Church. They are, therefore, Schismatics, and teach Heresies.'

Mr Baylee further informs his "Romanist friends", first that "The present creed of the Church of Rome was not the creed of the Catholic church for 1500 years after Christ. She has, therefore departed from the true faith." Secondly, that "No Catholic writer or Church for the first 200 years after Christ, taught the adoration of the Host, transubstantiation, the invocation of departed Saints, the worship of the Blessed Virgin, the forced celibacy of the clergy, or the necessity of auricular confession" and, thirdly, that "the doctrines of the Roman church, so far as different from those of the Anglo-Catholic Church, are contrary to God's word." The Reverend gentleman thus subscribes his placard:

"As Christ's lawfully appointed minister towards you, I subscribe myself, in grave truth, Your friend in Him, Joseph Baylee A.M. Priest of the one Catholic and Apostolic Church, and principal of the Birkenhead Theological College."

The pious soul of the *Mail* claps Mr Baylee on the back, and this graciously throws the shield of his favour, to a certain extent, over the poor benighted Roman Catholics: "We have a certain respect for hereditary Roman Catholics from appreciation of deference to parents and to spiritual pastors. But we have no patience with those apostate simpletons,

> who, because of lamented defects in our communion, plunge, as it were, out of the frying pan into the fire, and by way of intense religion, violate God's express commands, by 'bowing down' to wooden images and waxwork dolls! Whenever Romanists would insidiously rob us of our title to being Catholic, we break silence -otherwise, on our settled conviction that any religion, any form of Christianity, is infinitely better than none, we always rejoice that since so few of the poor are to be seen in our own churches, crowds of them, at least, flock to Roman Catholic chapels." if we are to believe the Roman Catholics themselves, they do *not* worship either "wooden images" or "waxwork dolls", Or even "the Blessed Virgin", and as they ought to know their own beliefs and practices best, the repetition of the charge of idolatry against them would seem to involve a breach of that commandment which forbids us to bear false witness against our neighbour. But, *quote* the Roman Catholics, such breach seems to be a special privilege of special "Catholic" saints of the *Mail* and Baylee school of Christians.[53]

By the late 1840s the Catholic Irish of Birkenhead were well aware that they had an enemy, perhaps an agent provocateur, living among them. The influx of people escaping the Irish famine from 1847 onwards, meant that most of the people living around Holy Trinity Church were now Catholic. Oak Street had a population which was over 90% Irish Catholic. This was by no means a docile population. Indeed, they sometimes showed they could organise, resist and fight - even if it was, at times, among themselves.

The intention of the framers of the Poor Law, was that poor people should be isolated and stigmatised, as poor people often are nowadays. However, for the Irish poor, poverty was normal. They were not ashamed of their poverty. Everyone they knew was in the same boat. de Tocqueville spoke to an Irish priest in Ireland about

---

[53] Liverpool Mercury, 25th December, 1849

poverty in that country:

> Do you not know the aristocracy is the cause of all our miseries and that they do not alleviate any of the evils that they give rise to? Do you know Sir, what prevents the poor man of dying of hunger in Ireland? In Ireland, Sir, it is the poor who provide for the needs of the poor, it is the poor who raise and maintain the schools where the children of the poor are brought up, it is the poor finally who furnish the poor with the means of obtaining the comforts of religion. A farmer who has only 30 acres and who gathers only 100 bushels of potatoes, puts aside a fifth of his harvest to distribute annually to those unfortunates who are the most in need. The starving man presents himself without fear at the door of the thatched cottages; he is sure to receive something to appease his pressing hunger. But at the door of the mansions, he will meet only liveried lackeys or dogs better fed than he, who drive him harshly away. In order to give alms, the farmer will spare the manure for his field, his wife will sleep on straw, and his children will not go to school. What does the Lord do during all this time? He strolls in his vast estate surrounded by great walls. in the enclosure of his park everything breeds splendour, outside poverty groans, but he does not notice it. His doormen are careful to remove the poor man from his view, or if he meets him by chance he responds to his entreaties, 'I make it a duty not to encourage begging.' He has big and fat dogs, and his fellow creatures die at his door. Not only does he not relieve the needs of the poor in any way, but he profits from those needs by drawing enormous rent and goes to spend in France or in Italy the money thus acquired. If he returns for a short time among us, it is to evict from his estate a farmer who is behind in his rent and evict him from

his dwelling.[54]

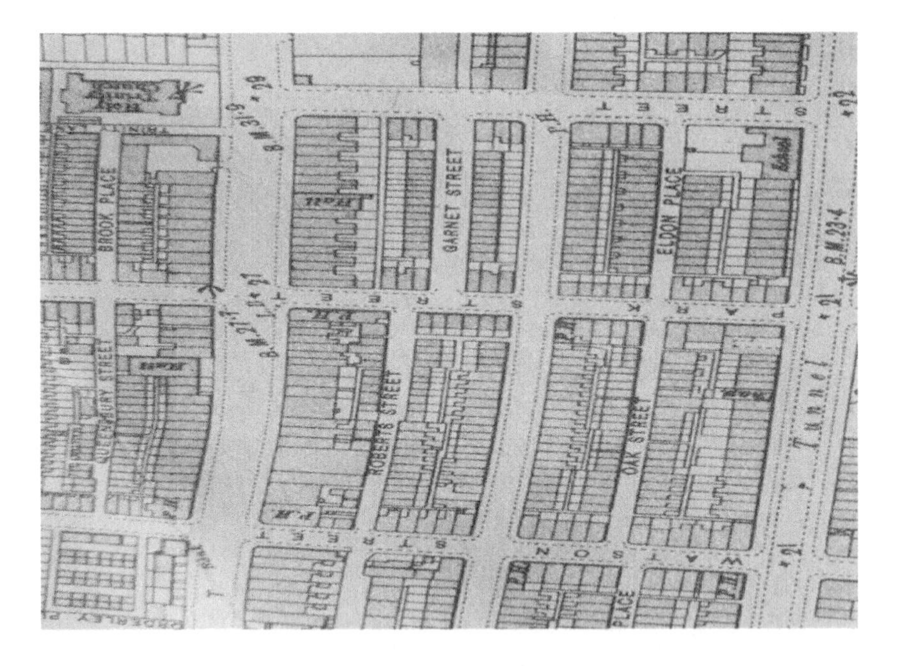

The streets around Holy Trinity Church[55]

[54] De Tocqueville, op. cit, pp. 116-117

[55] Ordnance Survey map of Birkenhead, 1909

CHAPTER FIVE

Papal Aggression

It is with this background that disturbances about religious issues in Birkenhead in the 1850s must be understood. On the one hand was an English Protestant population with deep suspicions of the Catholic Church and its ambitions and especially suspicious of Catholic priests. There was deep suspicion of Catholic institutions, convents especially. The Faithful Companions of Jesus opened a small convent in Hampton Street in Birkenhead in 1852, moving to Holt Hill in 1856. The Protestant population were being fed stories by an anti-Catholic press and by a clergy in the town which supported the Orange Order. On the other hand, there was a Catholic Irish immigrant population which was predisposed to being unruly, who were being goaded by Protestant clerics. The North End of Birkenhead was ready to explode at any time, because of faction disputes, because of labour problems or because of insults to Catholicism.

M'Neile had founded in Liverpool a militantly anti Catholic Tory Party, the same was being organised in Birkenhead. Tories, then and now, love to be outraged, hence the sales of the Daily Mail, and if they can be outraged by immigrants with a 'foreign' religion, so much the better. A perfect excuse for exhibiting outrage came in the closing months of 1850. The Pope,

Pius IX, decided that the Catholic Church in Great Britain had grown so rapidly with Irish immigration, that bishops should be appointed. There already were Catholic bishops in Ireland, supposedly a part of the United Kingdom.

Ultra-Protestants in Britain declared that this was a part of a dastardly papist plot to take over the British Empire and ultimately the whole world. What was essentially an administrative adjustment within the Catholic church, came to be represented as something far more sinister. Mass meetings were held in towns and cities all over the country. Generally, the meetings agreed to send addresses to Queen Victoria, the head of the Church of England, that she must resist papal aggression. Birkenhead went along with the rest of the country, except that in Birkenhead there was an opportunity to goad the town's Catholic population. A notice appeared on walls in the town:

> PUBLIC NOTICE
> We, the undersigned, acting in and for the Hundred of Wirral, in the county of Chester, having received a requisition, numerously and respectably signed, requesting us to call a public meeting in Birkenhead, for the purpose of presenting a loyal address to Her Majesty, praying her to take such measures as in her wisdom she may think fit effectually to resist the encroachments of Rome, in compliance therewith, do hereby convene a public meeting of the ratepayers of Birkenhead and its vicinity, and do appoint the same to be held in the town hall of Birkenhead, on Wednesday, November 27, at one o'clock in the afternoon.
> Richard Congreve, J.R. Clegg, Henry Winch, Wm Jackson, John Dean Chase Edward Cust, Jos. C. Ewart, J.S. Jackson, J.R. Shaw, William Hall.[56]

The intention behind the notice was clear. It was to criticise the Pope and to request the Queen to respond to him. The problem the magistrates had was that a third of the population of the town would react badly to that criticism. The magistrates wanted to call the meeting in such a way that Catholics were excluded. The first move was to call only ratepayers to the meeting. It was a legally dubious move to invite only ratepayers to a meeting described as 'public'. Most

[56] Liverpool Mercury, November 29th, 1850

Catholics were not ratepayers, but several hundred were.

A further move to exclude Catholics, was to call the 'public' meeting at the town hall, in which only about two hundred people could be accommodated. A confrontation had been set up, and duly came about.

Father Browne, the parish priest of St Werburgh's was the acknowledged leader of the Catholic community in Birkenhead. By now, most Catholics in the town were poor Irish. The poor Irish of Birkenhead were an unruly lot. Hundreds of them were hardened street fighters. They were devoted to the Catholic church and Father Browne, and they were unlikely to accept any insult to either, or to the Pope. They tended to think that putting in windows, when there was no personal injury to anyone, was a legitimate form of protest.

They could organise themselves, whether in factions, as proto-trade unions in defence of their work, in peaceful marching, in conducting and picketing strikes or in defending themselves against police brutality. They had their own speakers to address them when they were taking action. All of this with no clerical input, and often against clerical advice.

According to the Mercury account, crowds began to gather outside the town hall early in the morning of the proposed meeting. By ten o'clock there were thousands in the square. The crowd was peaceful until half past eleven, when the Liverpool police came out of the town hall and attacked members of the crowd. The crowd dispersed but came back half an hour later, this time armed with cudgels and sticks and proceeded to attack the police. The police then retreated into the town hall.

Towards one o'clock, people started entering the meeting. The majority were turned back by police at the door. Stone throwing began. The front of the town hall was stoned, and windows broken. The assembly room was in the back of the town hall.

The magistrates were gathered in a room at the front of the building. Most of them retreated into the Assembly Room. William Jackson called for Father Browne to calm the situation. Browne stepped through a shattered window and immediately the stone throwing stopped. Father Browne then invited the crowd to follow him and Mr Bretherton back to St Werburgh's Church. The magistrates, some of whom wanted to call in the military, others to issue the police with cutlasses, then decided to call off the meeting.

> TO THE INHABITANTS OF BIRKENHEAD AND ITS VICINITY
>
> Fellow Townsmen: After the unexpected occurrences which have taken place this morning, we consider it to be our duty to address a few words to you.
>
> You are well aware that a meeting of the ratepayers of Birkenhead and its vicinity was to have been held today, to express its opinion upon what is called "the recent papal aggression," or in other words, it was intended, by a small section of virulent and bigoted persons, that a meeting should be held to insult the Catholic religion. Such a proceeding, coupled with the language which had notoriously been used at similar meetings elsewhere, was calculated to excite to the utmost pitch the indignation of the mass of our Catholic residents.
>
> We venture to ask you, what would have been your feelings if our pastors had called a public meeting to insult the Archbishop of Canterbury and the rest of the English Bishops? This feeling of indignation very naturally led to the attendance at the place of meeting of large numbers of the Catholic population. They were not able to conceive that the Public Authorities would call a meeting to which ratepayers only would be admitted, and thus attempt to exclude the humbler classes, who, upon a question affecting their religion, have as much right to be heard as the magistrates themselves. To their utter surprise, however, although the place of the meeting was not half filled, and that principally by policemen, not a man was admitted to the room who was not dressed in broad cloth.
>
> At about half past eleven, whilst the people were quietly awaiting admission into the room, a most unprovoked and wanton attack was made upon them

by a party of Liverpool police, who had, very unwisely, been called to the place of meeting. Many of us are able to testify, of our own knowledge, to the fact that unoffending parties were thus struck and furiously beaten, when no provocation had been given by anyone. Such attacks were repeatedly made, without cause, during the morning. Some of the police force was stationed inside the building, to examine every individual who passed in, as to whether he was a Ratepayer. Numerous Catholic and others were excluded all together from what was alleged to be a public meeting, and so called by the magistrates. That the people, under these circumstances, have defended themselves from their assailants, and should even have been excited to retaliatory violence by this treatment, is not to be wondered at; and we think that every reasonable man will concur with us in attributing the whole blame to the bigots who called the meeting in the first instance, to the grossly injudicious manner In which the arrangements were made, and to the wanton and uncalled for attacks made by the police upon the people.

To the exertions of Catholic gentlemen, headed by their revered clergyman, it is alone due to them that the excitement was so soon allayed. They only were active in the efforts to appease it and expose their persons to imminent peril whilst the Magistrates, with the single exception of Mr John Jackson, shrunk from their duty, and retired into a sheltered room.

We make this statement to you, because we have reason to apprehend that, with the usual fairness of the parties opposed to us, the facts will be distorted and untruly represented. We cannot conclude our address to you without expressing our perfect willingness, at any moment, to attend a public meeting of the inhabitants of Birkenhead, if such a one shall be called, to discuss calmly the question now in agitation, and we entertain a very strong opinion that we shall be able to convince such a meeting that the outrage raised against us is unwarrantable, discreditable to the English people, and a gross outrage on the principles of civil and religious liberty.[57]

The placard was signed by Father Browne, Mr Bretherton and seventeen of the town's leading Catholics. In a conciliatory gesture, Father Browne posted another placard asking Catholics to keep away from any further public meeting on the issue.

TO THE CATHOLICS OF BIRKENHEAD

Fellow Catholics: Another meeting has been summoned to meet in this town, on Friday, to give public expression on a fact which is called an act of papal aggression.

On occasion of a recent similar meeting, you all well know and can testify to the peaceable spirit and goodwill which animated our body and induced us all to attend. You equally know, and in common lament, the sad and unforeseen disturbance that then occurred; and you have all since had grave and painful cause to feel bitterly the public odium and gratuitous calumnies which our fellow townsmen, some it is to be feared, maliciously, and many more, doubtlessly from misrepresentation, have thrown upon us. Neither Christian humility nor Christian charity have gained by the late excitement of angry words and sectarian prejudice; neither can I close my eyes to the fact that new parties have originated this movement, that the notice convening the meeting is not restricted to the inhabitants of Birkenhead, but is convened in terms that includes all parts of the country, and the public press has pressed the necessity of attendance upon all Protestant friends in

57 Ibid

> Cheshire, as if for the express purpose of overwhelming us with numbers and clamour rather than causing arguments and amicable discussion. No resolution passed in your absence, and by a meeting so assembled, can possibly be construed into an expression of opinions of the inhabitants of Birkenhead, of whom you form so large a part.
>
> Further, it is well known that an enquiry into the late disturbances has been demanded of Sir George Grey on behalf of the Catholics of Birkenhead, pending which any untoward events, such as appears to be anticipated by the magistrates themselves, will readily be seized upon to implicate us, and used as an argument in support of unfounded and calumnious assertions. Under these circumstances rather than risk a further disparagement of the two essential principles of the Christian religion I have before named, it seems to me a thousand times preferable to bear patiently, and in silence, the proclamation of any body of our mistaken countrymen of a public charge against us, of which we feel ourselves, as loyal and good citizens, quite incapable.
>
> I beg, therefore, to request of the Catholic body that they will individually and collectively absent themselves from attendance at such meeting, Trust, with me, that time and more mature reflection on the part of our fellow citizens will, in the merciful dispensation of divine providence, intend to assuage the spirit of irritation that has been evoked, and render more condign justice to the feelings and intentions by which we are governed and influenced.
>
> EDWARD F. BROWNE
>
> Presbytery of St Werburgh's, Dec 11, 1850.[58]

The Protestant response was predictable, the Liverpool Mail wrote of Father Browne:

---

[58] Liverpool Mercury, December 11th, 1850

> He has the impudence to advise the magistrates of Birkenhead to call a meeting of Protestants, in which case his impudence says, "none of our people will interfere." Does this not show by whom 'our people' were induced to interfere?
>
> Such power in a priest, over an ignorant and enslaved rabble, is obnoxious to every principle of British and constitutional liberty.[59]

The promised meeting did take place on Friday 13th of December 1850. The level of security against attack was astonishing. The public meeting was held in the market square, behind the old market. The speakers' platform was guarded by one thousand special constables armed with staves. The Birkenhead and Wirral police were in the square, with three hundred Liverpool police on call to take the ferry, should they be needed. On top of all this, there were three hundred troops in the market hall itself. This can be seen as a rehearsal for the so-called Garibaldi riots of 1862. John Laird chaired the proceedings. the crowd numbered between six and seven thousand. Various speakers used the security thus guaranteed, to roundly insult the Pope, Romish Bishops and Catholicism in general. Mr Percy Dove may serve as an example:

> Be it enacted, that from and after the passing of this act, any Roman priest who shall take to himself the title of Bishop of any portion of Her Majesty's dominions shall be considered to have forfeited his rights and privileges as a British subject, and shall be dealt with as a foreigner, who has grossly violated and set at nought the laws of the realm. And be it further enacted, that from and after this, any such priest who shall have been shown to have committed the above offence shall be with all possible dispatch embarked in a ship of War of Her Majesty's (cheers) and be landed at some port in Italy, which shall be

[59] Liverpool Mail, 7th Dec, 1850

> conveniently near to the capital of the foreign prelate to whom he has by the said offence declared his allegiance" (cheers). The operation of this would be, supposing priest Brown when inducted into the see of Birkenhead, he would immediately have him shipped off, and supposing he were to come round the continent, and arrive there again, after giving him a week for refreshments and to recover from the effects of the sea voyage, he would see him off again. The effect of this would be in the short time the whole papal hierarchy, both in England and Ireland, would be continually on their travels (cheers), they would not reach the dignity of martyrs; and after a walk over Europe for three or four years, there would be an end of the papal hierarchy.[60]

Birkenhead's leading Church of England cleric, Rev. A. Knox, vicar of St. Mary's also contributed:

> It was my own anxious wish not to come forward on this occasion, not from any feelings of friendship towards the Pope of Rome, or towards the Pope's measures, because I have been able to make my solemn protest against him and his measures in the town hall (hear, hear), the very week before that melancholy assault took place. I grieve when I think of it, that English Protestants, met together to enjoy their privileges, as Englishmen were assaulted, and if God had not interposed, probably a great portion of us would have been murdered. My desire, with reference to this meeting, was that the laity alone should come forward and manifest that true spirit of Englishmen, and Protestants, which is which it is so abundantly manifesting. But I have given way to the requests and entreaties of the committee who have had the management of this meeting, from the

---

[60] Liverpool Mail, December 14th, 1850

position I hold in Birkenhead, being now one of the oldest inhabitants in the place, having for three and twenty years, with God's blessing, being able to reside among you as a peaceable citizen, but especially as the spiritual head of this place. I have given way to the request of the committee, and have come forward here this day, not to occupy your time at any length, but to utter my solemn protest, in the hearing of this assembly and, against the insult which has been offered to our beloved Queen upon the throne, and to all her subjects (hear, hear). We are not together this day to contend for that which is dear to every man, but especially to Britons - civil and religious liberty. Thank God! we enjoy it, both Protestants and Roman Catholics - we enjoy civil and religious liberty under the benign sway of our protestant constitution, and our beloved Protestant Queen Victoria (cheers). The Pope of Rome, a foreign prince, has dared to invade her dominions with his bull, (great laughter) and endeavoured to wrest from her hands that sceptre which she, in the fear of God, sways over her blessed dominions. He has, as you are aware, parcelled out her kingdom into dioceses for his archbishops, and bishops he wishes to place over them, if we will allow him, (hear, hear) his sworn servants, to carry out his wishes, his canon laws; to enslave our Queen, and enslave her subjects, both Protestant and Roman Catholic. Let Roman Catholics understand this: My fellow townsmen in Birkenhead, who are Roman Catholics, you are little aware of the attempts to enslave you as well as Protestants. (A voice: "It's true.") You don't understand the canon law of Rome; the canon law of Rome is the system of the most dire slavery wherever it may be put in force. (Hear, hear.)[61]

---

[61] Ibid

The meeting went off peacefully. In the name of 'free speech', militant Protestants had been enabled to insult their Catholic neighbours. The phrase 'free speech' had traditionally been associated with a cause supporting the powerless against the powerful. Tory governments from 1819 to 1855 taxed newspapers, to keep them out of the hands of the working class. Conservatives believed that a radical working class had to be suppressed - and they were denied 'free speech' by Tory governments. In Birkenhead in 1859 Conservatives were co-opting the language of 'free speech' to attack the powerless, and especially Irish Catholics who were systematically denied a voice.

The lesson that John Laird, as Chairman of the Improvement Commission that ran the town, and the Birkenhead magistrates learned, was that to keep Catholics quiet while they were insulted, they needed either a cooperative Catholic clergyman or massive force, but preferably both. The Liverpool Mercury carried some interesting editorial comment:

> In particular localities, and at particular times, it may, however, be far more efficacious and prudent for the leading men to summon a meeting of the friends of a cause, than to call upon the authorities to convene a public meeting. Had the Protestants of Birkenhead, for instance, themselves called a meeting of all who were opposed to papal aggression, the largest room in the town might easily have been filled; the opponents would have had no right to be present; the proceedings would have gone off in a peaceable manner; a disgraceful riot would have been prevented; life and property would not have been placed in danger; much money would have been saved; apprehension would have been kept down, and a great deal of angry and bitter feeling would never have been roused. To this course the Roman Catholic population could not possibly have objected, because they themselves would have had the right to call a counter-meeting and to pass counter-resolutions.
>
> On a question which has to a very considerable

extent assumed a religious character, such a course of procedure would have been far more graceful, kindly, and wise, than if the object in view you had been purely political, and it would certainly have been quite as influential. but we are sorry to say that the Protestants of Birkenhead, seemed to have no conception whatever of exercising their faculty in the spirit of noble forbearance and charity. After the first meeting had, to say the least, been improperly called and provokingly managed, and after this conduct had produced a serious breach of the peace, they nevertheless persisted in carrying out the object in their own way, no matter what might be the result. Virtually they declared to the world that there should be a public meeting in Birkenhead, even though it led to a collision in which scores of lives might be sacrificed. Hundreds of special constables were enrolled, and hundreds of police officers were borrowed, until an armed force was mustered equal in strength to that of the expected enemy. Had not the Roman Catholics manifested a commendable forbearance, there might have been gathered in the marketplace, some two thousand men, half of them armed with batons, and the other half with sticks and bludgeons, in order to decide the important question whether the meeting should not have been a special instead of a public one. Protestant clergyman and Protestant gentlemen, for a mere form, imperilled human life and property. Really, this was not wise; this was no manifestation of a Christian feeling. Had there been no other mode than by "public" meeting in which the Protestant inhabitants of Birkenhead could have given full expression to their sentiments, then we should have been inclined to say, "Let such a meeting be held, at all costs. Let not the exercise of a great public privilege be interdicted by a part only of the community …" But this was not the case. there was another way in which

> the demonstration might have been made quite as effectively - more in accordance with true religious feelings, and, and if we mistake not, more in harmony with those laws of custom which regulate such assemblages in Great Britain.[62]

Father Browne had predicted that Catholics would be represented as the villains of the piece, and this was certainly the case in the minds of many Protestants and in the Tory press. The Liverpool Mail wrote:

> The murderous proceedings of an Irish and popish mob at Birkenhead, on Wednesday last, will surely convince all Englishman of the painful but stern duty which now devolves upon them. To resist popery, illustrated as it is by the deeds of popery at Birkenhead, is to resist, suppress, or punish crime. The Pope has invaded England - he must be driven back and rendered incapable of ever committing a similar aggression on this country. An Irish Mob of ignorant and savage papists, employed as labourers in this country, interfere with the just and inalienable rights and privileges of Englishman, called together for a legal and peaceful purpose, and act the part of hired but frantic assassins - they must be driven back too!
>
> It appears that the magistrates of the Hundred of Wirral call the public meeting of the ratepayers of Birkenhead, to take into the consideration the conduct of the bishop of Rome, in assuming new and unheard of power and spiritual jurisdiction in this realm of England. At or before the time of holding the meeting, some two or three thousand of these Irish labourers, not one man in one hundred of whom can possibly be ratepayers, presented themselves in a body before the Town hall. They were almost all armed with bludgeons, staves, pokers, iron bars, and

---

[62] Liverpool Mercury, 17th Dec, 1850

> afterwards with iron rails, plundered for the purpose - all being instruments of death or destruction.
>
> ... It is necessary, however, that the Protestants of this part of the country should know that the ferocious attack at Birkenhead was the work of priests, or some other powerful instigation. We all know the influence which a popish priest has in Ireland, over the ignorant peasants in that country. There is no crime which the priest, in the sister island, cannot induce one or more of his superstitious slaves to commit, provided he can identify the crime with the advancement of what is called religion.
>
> It will be seen that this was attempted, perhaps only by an assumed agency or a second hand, at Birkenhead. The assembling of the Irish labourers, who are called Englishmen, and who had no right to be present at the meeting at all, was done under the mask of religion. Now, what is an ignorant papist's religion? The Irish Workmen at the Birkenhead docks cannot possibly have the slightest or any correct motion of the merits or objects of the Pope's bull. What they know, if they know anything at all, they must have learnt in their chapels, where almost everything that is there told them is false. If they had been told that the Pope wished to establish territorial bishops in England, and that the Queen, the ministry, the English church, and the Protestant population, were opposed to the scheme, is it likely that an Irish labourer, who can neither read nor write, would have cared one straw about a proposition so much above his comprehension? If these workmen had only been told this, this and nothing more, there would have been no bludgeon riot, no destruction of property, no shedding of blood, at Birkenhead.[63]

Three days later, at two o'clock in the morning, five people were

[63] Liverpool Mail, Dec. 14th, 1850

arrested for participating in the original riots of 27th of November. The trial of the five accused took place at Chester Assizes in April 1851. It is worth noting that a significant aspect of Orange discourse, the argument that Catholics were always ready to accept direction by priests, was used to persuade jurors of the guilt of the men accused. Fairly predictably, the prosecution went for the line that the prisoners in the dock were engaged in a plot to prevent the meeting happening at all. The centre of the plot was Father Browne, the evil genius who was in absolute control of a crowd of poor, stupid Irishmen. The prosecutor argued:

> In the morning of 27th November, a large party of the lower orders of Irish, not ratepayers, got possession of the town hall as early as half past nine o'clock, and that is was with great difficulty that they could be got out, though it was then three hours before the time of the meeting. At a later period of the day, about half past eleven o'clock, several hundred of the Irish labourers had assembled in front of the town hall, and there could be no doubt that that crowd, at a nod of the priest's head, or the movement of his finger, could have been induced to do whatever Father Browne listed. The priest well knew the feelings of the people; he saw that mischief was brewing, but he took no steps to nip it in the bud, or to carry the crowd away, but allowed them to remain on the spot until the disturbance began. It was clear, then, that Father Browne's determination was either to fill the meeting with those who were not ratepayers, and who had no business there, or to prevent the meeting from being held; and in the latter object he no doubt succeeded.[64]

John Roebuck, a Radical lawyer and MP, defended some of the prisoners. He also alleged there was a plot. The plotters, however, were not Irish, they were the magistrates of Birkenhead.

---

[64] Chester Chronicle, 12th April, 1851

> But what were the facts? These gentlemen (the magistrates) received a requisition to convene a meeting of the "inhabitants" of the town; but instead of doing so, they convened a meeting of another class. Why, these men did all in their power to excite ill-will twixt man and man, and in pursuance of this object all that had arisen of an evil character had arisen in consequence of these gentlemen's departure from the terms of the requisition of the inhabitants of Birkenhead, by disregarding the requisition for a meeting of the "inhabitants" and calling a meeting of the "ratepayers" of Birkenhead and its vicinity. He in the course of his worldly career had had some experience in calling public meetings, and he knew what was intended. He charged these gentlemen, the magistrates, with the direct, the concocted, and the deliberate intention of packing the meeting. They wanted to get a meeting of their own followers under the guise of a meeting of the people of Birkenhead, and he told them that they had done their utmost to pack that meeting. He charged them with a deliberate attempt to pack the meeting, intending, after they had packed it, to represent to her Majesty that this meeting represented the feelings spontaneously expressed of the great body of the inhabitants dwelling in that town.[65]

Five of the six prisoners were found guilty of riot, two were sentenced to a year in prison and three to nine months. The jury were sufficiently sceptical of police evidence that they recommended that the prisoners although guilty should be treated mercifully. The judge also criticised the police:

> His Lordship, in passing sentence, said he thought it right to say that the conduct of the police, on the

---

[65] Ibid

> occasion of the first disturbance, was, in his opinion, not only injudicious but unjustifiable, by reason of taking too peremptory and too active measures to remove the people from the front of the town hall. He was not surprised at this irritating the crowd.[66]

Roebuck continued to pursue their case after the trial. His arguments found some credence at the Home Office. The prisoners were granted a Royal Pardon in June 1851. The Catholic Newspaper, The Tablet, announced the pardoning of the prisoners in July of that year:

> Those men, as our readers are aware, were thrown into prison on the pretence of being to blame for the disturbance at the Birkenhead no-popery meeting, which disturbance was, in fact, caused by a savage and unprovoked attack on the part of the Protestants. They were manacled as felons, dragged as such through Birkenhead and Chester, and after, on the evidence of the police (the parties mainly to blame), were convicted by the Protestant jury, and sentenced to prison. They have since been set at liberty, through the exertions of the Defence Committee, and at the recommendation of Sir G. Grey.[67]

---

[66] Ibid

[67] The Tablet, 5th July, 1851

CHAPTER SIX

Birkenhead Cemetery Riots: John Laird and Canon Chapman – Enemies to Allies

John Laird[68]

[68] John Laird, National Portrait Gallery

For Irish Catholics, cemeteries were a uniquely sensitive subject. The Church of Ireland took over Irish Catholic churches during the Reformation. They also took over the graveyards which were attached to them.

The traditional practice of Irish Catholics was that the dead should be buried with their ancestors, and their bones should mingle with those of their forefathers. Irish Catholics therefore needed access to Protestant graveyards. However, from the 1820s many Church of Ireland clergymen were on the offensive. There was a militant Evangelical Crusade against the supposed evils of Catholicism. As a part of this "second Reformation", of which M'Neile and Baylee were a part, some Church of Ireland vicars decided not to allow a Catholic priest to officiate, or even say prayers, at gravesides.

This was meat and drink to Daniel O'Connell and his Catholic Association, who wanted home rule for Ireland. They were enabled to portray vicars of the Church of Ireland as heartless and ruthless, as, indeed, many were. For them the Irish peasantry were ignorant, superstitious, and priest-ridden, little better than brutes.

By 1859 the population of Birkenhead had grown to about thirty-five thousand. There were insufficient places in churchyards to bury Birkenhead's dead. Protestant control of a cemetery was not likely to be a popular choice for the Irish population of the town. John Laird, as chairman of the Improvement Commission, which ran Birkenhead, decided to call an election for ratepayers of the town. The electorate were asked to choose between two options; one was an independent burial board. This was the proposal of Mr Craven, a dissenter by background. The other option was that the cemetery should be run by the Improvement Commission itself.

The Irish Catholic population was probably influenced by the fact that John Laird was notoriously an Orangeman, and that the workforce of his shipyard was entirely Protestant. The situation was not helped by the fact that John Laird had commissioned several horse-drawn buses to travel through the town to take supporters to the polls. The buses had bands on the upper deck playing Orange airs. Orange airs, like Orange parades, are Invariably triumphalist, proclaiming Orange superiority. The scene was set for a riot. A riot duly broke out, although it was to have a surprising ending. The Liverpool Mercury published the following account:

> THE CEMETERY QUESTION AT BIRKENHEAD
>
> Riotous proceedings - Close of the poll
>
> The polling on the question of a cemetery for Birkenhead was resumed on Tuesday morning, at eight o'clock, amidst great excitement. 3000 or 4000 thousand people, consisting principally of dock labourers, congregated early in front of the Town Hall, and fears were entertained that a breach of the peace would ensue. The shops in the principal thoroughfares of the township were closed, and business operations were completely suspended. A large body of navvies favourable to Mr Craven's motion to have a burial board irrespective of the commissioners, but very few of whom possessed votes, were determined, if possible, to carry the point by intimidation and violence. Having armed themselves with heavy bludgeons and other weapons they repaired to the dock and other works and drove away those men who were peaceably inclined and who did not want to take part in the disgraceful proceedings. At ten o'clock about a thousand of these ruffians, many of whom seemed to be in a state bordering on intoxication, marched from the North End of the township to the front of the Town Hall, all yelling and shouting in a furious manner. The police however succeeded for a time in maintaining tranquillity. The Reverend Canon Chapman, the Reverend G. B. Clegg, and the Reverend Joseph Daly (of the Catholic Chapel, Grange Lane), along with Mr Edward Bretherton, solicitor, also used every exertion to prevent an outbreak and ultimately succeeded in disarming a portion of the mob of the cudgels, some of which were taken into the police office, while nearly a cartload were removed to the Catholic

chapel house. At one time the state of things appeared so alarming that it was under contemplation to send to Chester for the military, but this idea was subsequently abandoned. A company of the marines belonging to HMS Hastings, under the command of Lieutenant Robilliard, who had been ashore exercising, were communicated with, and they marched through Hamilton Square, with bayonets pointed. This had the effect of dispersing a large number of those who were riotously disposed.

During the whole of the forenoon, the polling was with great difficulty proceeded with, the entrance to the Town Hall being blocked up by the crowd. At one o'clock the numbers were: for Mr Craven's motion for the establishment of a burial board by the vestry, 719; for Mr Laird's amendment to request the commissioners to resolve themselves into a burial board, 1379; majority for Mister Laird's proposition, 660. Mr Craven announced his intention to withdraw his motion and expressed the hope that the commotion would immediately subside, and that the people would withdraw to their homes in a quiet and orderly manner. …

The Reverend Canon Chapman also stated that the Catholics had obtained all they wanted, and he earnestly entreated the mob to refrain from violence and to return peaceably to their homes.

The Town Hall was then cleared, but the mob appeared determined not to act upon the advice given to them by the Reverend Canon Chapman and other gentlemen. A few of the ringleaders were captured and lodged in bridewell. This seemed to exasperate them, and fierce and savage were the imprecations uttered by the infuriated navvies. Having been disarmed in the forenoon by the Catholic clergymen, the ruffians now felt themselves at a loss for weapons, but they were not long in procuring a fresh supply from the North End of the town.[69]

It would appear that Canon Chapman had gone for a tea break. In his absence, and the absence of other priests from St Werburgh's Church, traditional rivalries and hatreds asserted themselves. Perhaps people found it hard to believe that the town's leading Orangeman and the town's leading Catholic were cooperating.

> Armed a second time, the mob in great numbers made a furious attack upon the extensive ship-building premises of Mr Laird, the object being to provoke the numerous workmen in that gentleman's employ to an encounter. Mr Laird, we believe, had given strict orders to his men, not to mix themselves up with any disturbance, and consequently it was not until matters had assumed a serious aspect that any of them determined to remain passive no longer. Volleys of stones and other dangerous missiles were thrown over into the works; some windows at the north entrance to the premises were smashed, and ultimately one of the large doors forced open. The mob next made a rush into the yard; but they were met by a body of Mr Laird's men, armed with bars of iron. The fight was of short duration. The navvies could not stand the heavy metal of the workers in iron, and they fled in the greatest confusion to join their companions who were creating a disturbance in front of the Town Hall.[70]

Evidently word of all this had reached Canon Chapman. He reappeared at the town hall and played the leading role in defusing the whole situation, in which lives could well have been lost.

> The next object of the mob was to release the prisoners who were lodged in bridewell in the

[69] Liverpool Mercury, June 3rd, 1859

[70] Ibid

> forenoon. About four o'clock two or three attempts were made to reach this building, but the mob were held back by the Reverend Canon Chapman, who exposed himself to the greatest danger by going into the midst of the infuriated men and expostulated with them on the impropriety of their behaviour. At this time Mr Bryans and Mr Potter, magistrates, were in consultation. The police, to the number of about forty, were ready with their cutlasses to clear away the mob, but it is sad that, by the instruction of the magistrates, they were not allowed to show themselves, being apprehensive that loss of life would be the result. A third furious attack upon the bridewell led to a consultation between the magistrates and the Reverend Canon Chapman. The Reverend gentleman recommended that the prisoners should be released, he becoming responsible for their appearance to answer any charge preferred against them on the following day. Magistrate agreed to this proposal, and the prisoners were accordingly released, and to the cheers of crowds of men and women.[71]

The Dublin Weekly Nation added to its account of the rioting:

> A large crowd of people still remained discussing the serious turn affairs had taken, and the query of many was: "When we die, why should not we Catholics have prayers read over us by our priests and not by their parsons?[72]"

Cameron Chapman was the hero of the hour. But not only was he a hero, he had secured the most unlikely of alliances. He had obviously worked closely with John Laird in the days before the election. He had restored peace to the town and was continuing to collaborate with

---

[71] Ibid

[72] Dublin Weekly Nation, 11th June, 1859

John Laird to their mutual advantage and the advantage of Catholics of Birkenhead.

All of which, must have been galling to the Conservatives and Orangemen of Liverpool and Birkenhead; their view of the situation was expressed in a letter published in the Liverpool Mercury:

> THE KING OF BIRKENHEAD
>
> To the Editors of the Liverpool Mercury:
>
> Gentlemen, it would appear from the report of the disgraceful proceedings in today's Mercury that the Birkenhead magistrates are powerless, and that the sole authority in the preservation of order rests with the Reverend Canon Chapman, who ought at once to be proclaimed the civil and ecclesiastical Sovereign of Birkenhead. I hope that a memorial will be presented to the Home Secretary calling upon him to enquire into the conduct of the magistrates of Birkenhead, who in the most cowardly manner consented to the release of prisoners then in custody – the liberation being demanded by the threat of a papist crowd and urged by the Roman Catholic priest of the town. We are already beginning to experience the effects of the alliance between the Derby government and the Roman Catholics, and the audacious conduct of the ignorant mob at Birkenhead shows how meekly and justly the papists would exercise the power if ever they obtained it in this country. It may be argued that the priest urged the release of the prisoners for the sake of order, but what must be the moral effect upon a cloud of rioters when it is known that the priest has a power above the Queen's representatives? The magistrates who display such a want of dignity, of power, and of discretion ought at once to have their names erased from the justice roll. They were within a few minutes distance of Chester, whence they could have received a detachment of military. The marines and sailors from the Liffey and Hastings could have been had at a few minutes notice, and the police force

of Liverpool could have crossed the river immediately in order to restore order; and yet the weak minded, pusillanimous, chicken hearted magistrates of Birkenhead gave way to the threats of a few hundred rioters and at their bidding discharged from custody a set of scoundrels who deserve transportation. The magistrates of Birkenhead never stood very high in their opinion of their fellow townsmen; now their conduct will bring upon them the well merited contempt of all classes. – yours &c.

June 1st 1859 – A LOOKER ON[73]

John Laird's Election

Chapman – The Good Shepherd?

In December 1861 John Laird was elected as Birkenhead's first MP. The cooperation between Laird and Chapman had continued. Chapman spoke at several Laird's meetings and addressed crowds in Laird's support:

MEETING OF MR LAIRD'S FRIENDS

On Saturday afternoon, a meeting of the electors favourable to the return of Mr Laird was held at the Queen's Hotel, opposite the park entrance ... the Reverend Canon Chapman spoke in support of Mr Laird, whom he warmly eulogized as a friend to the poor, he and his family having enabled him (Canon Chapman) two or three times a week, for several weeks together, to give as many as eight hundred tickets for the relief of the poor. But for this timely and valuable assistance, the poor would in many instances have been starved, and many of the

[73] Liverpool Mercury, 2nd June, 1859

> children must have died. He moved a resolution expressive of Mr Laird's fitness to represent Birkenhead in Parliament.[74]

Canon Chapman was English and may well have been a Conservative all his life. Events in the early 1860s, However, were sufficient to attract him to the Conservative Party. The papacy was under attack. In the 1860s the Pope was not only a spiritual leader. The Papal States occupied much of central Italy, and Italian nationalist movements, whose military leader was Garibaldi, were seeking to overthrow Papal Rule and unite Italy as one nation. The Liberal Party tended to support nationalist movements, wherever they occurred, against old Empires and monarchies. The Conservative Party tended to be much more reactionary. In Italy in particular, the Conservative party supported the Pope.

In Birkenhead, Chapman set about mobilizing support for John Laird and the Tory Party. This was something of an uphill task. The big landowners in Ireland were Tory stalwarts. They were the least sympathetic to Irish grievances. Liberals, on the other hand, tended to be more attentive to Irish causes. Later in the 1860s, for instance, the Liberal Party disestablished the Church of Ireland. Catholics were no longer required to pay tithes for the upkeep of the Church. In 1870 they also passed a Land Act which took away some of landlords' powers of arbitrary eviction.

Another difficulty Chapman faced was that his Liberal opponent was Joseph Brassey. Thomas Brassey, his father, was Birkenhead's other major employer. He was the proprietor of the Canada Works in Birkenhead docklands and the world's biggest railway contractor and builder. It was in the Canada Works that Canada's first railway system was prefabricated, and railway equipment was built and exported all over the world. Brassey built a third of this country's railways. He built railways in France, Australia, South America, and India. In all his enterprises he insisted on taking on local partners. He employed Irish people, French people, Argentinians, and so on. His employment practises were in direct contrast to John Laird, who would employ

[74] Liverpool Mercury, 9th Dec, 1861

only Protestants.

The flavour of the opposition to both Chapman and Laird can perhaps be gauged by the following article, which appeared in the Cheshire Observer:

> THE TRADES UNIONISTS
>
> On Monday evening a very large meeting of the trades of Birkenhead was held at the theatre, for the purpose of "taking into consideration the relative claims to support the two candidates". Mr John Williams, a working man, occupied the chair. Mr Connolly, one of a deputation from London, a Catholic and an Irishman, in supporting a resolution in favour of an extension of the franchise, delivered a long speech, in the course of which he said he was sorry to see Roman Catholics coalescing with Orangemen in opposing liberalism. He denied the right of Canon Chapman or any other canon in England, to coerce or hand over the Irish Catholic inhabitants of this country to their ancient hereditary foes, the Tories, the men who ruled the country by pitch cap and triangles.[75]

[75] Cheshire Observer, 14th Dec, 1861

Captain Swayne Pitchcapping the People of Prosperous[76]

He denied the right of Canon Chapman to coerce any man to record his vote for that rank Tory, Mr Laird. It was the first time in the history of the Catholic church he had ever seen or read of a Grandmaster of an Orange Lodge and a pastor of a Catholic flock combining to defeat liberalism. There was no Catholic breathing who had a greater respect for his clergymen on the altar and in the sanctuary than he had; but when once they meddled with politics, they

[76] A 1798 cartoon, Prosperous Heritage Society, accessed Oct 19th, 2020

> were only men, and the power was not allocated to them to influence their flocks to vote contrary to their consciences and their interests. (Loud cheers.)[77]

Three days before the election, Canon Chapman called a meeting of selected Catholics to the schoolroom attached to St Werburgh's church. The reporter from the Cheshire Observer was not allowed into the meeting but he recorded what preceded the meeting and what went on outside. Four Catholic priests were present; the Reverend Canon Chapman, the Reverend J Rogerson, the Rev. R. W. Brundritt, and the Rev. E. Buguet, all of whom were English.

> Long before eight o'clock, the hour for commencing business, a very large number of Catholics had assembled in front of the building; but only a few who possessed circulars were admitted, which created great discontent, and caused many to denounce the whole affair in no measured terms exclaiming, "it was our money bought the place, and we must get in." Police constables, however, guarded the entrance, and prevented all from getting in without them possessing the circular, and the interior was guarded by the priests; but for some time, a breach of the peace was anticipated. There were loud shouts of "Brassey forever," and the whole assembly appeared to be much in favour of the Liberal candidate. Soon after eight o'clock the Reverend Canon Chapman and three other priests, accompanied by Mr Bretherton arrived, and then it appeared that some persons who had not received a circular had gained admission. Those having been pointed out to the Reverend Canon Chapman, a contemporary described what took place: "A few of those who were in favour of Mr Brassey appeared to have managed to get into the rooms by means of circulars, which had been addressed to other persons.

---

[77] Cheshire Observer, 14th Dec, 1861

These interlopers were immediately pointed out to the Reverend Canon Chapman, who at once ordered them to leave the room. Having shown some reluctance to quit their seats, the Reverend Canon, who is a strong powerful man, speedily resorted to physical force, and seized one after another of the delinquents by the back of the neck, he ejected them from the building. Resistance on the part of the "Brasseyites" was useless, and those who were in favour of the Liberal candidate seemed to be quite disconcerted in the presence of their pastors. The scene outside was rather alarming, many with circulars and many without demanding admission, amongst whom was Mr William Milner, who exercised considerable influence over the crowd, but all appeals were in vain. Mr Milner, now, addressed those assembled outside, and that to great applause, and in the course of his remarks denounced the meeting then being held in the schoolroom to be packed. It was, he said, something like the old, packed juries of Ireland. Mr Bretherton, and those gentlemen connected with him, had met to advocate the cause of Mr Laird, the Tory candidate, but he (Mr Milner) should ever use all his exertions in the cause of reform. He was devotedly attached to the Catholic Church, and he had made three attempts to get into the school room. It was most unfair that he should be excluded.... he called upon them to exercise their votes according to their conscience.... he for one could not enter the Tory fold. The Tories, for upwards of two centuries, had been keeping down the poor working people of poor old Ireland. There was a system that has bound her people in chains ... those who knew him would know that he was a good Catholic, and that he entertained the highest respect for the clergy. He held, however, that the moment a priest left the sanctuary of the Lord and entered into the area of politics, then he became public property

> and was open to comment like any other man ... when they stepped into politics then they became as fallible as he was.[78]

Something about what happened after the meeting, was revealed by the Liverpool Mercury on the day after the election:

> The Reverend Canon Chapman and the three other Roman Catholic priests of Birkenhead were won to the Tory side, not as mere supporters, but as active and powerful champions. The canon, in fact, proved himself to be a great gun. He called together a meeting of the Catholic voters, from which the refractory and independent members of the body were either expelled by brute force or kept away by ignorance of the assemblage, and the canon exploded in a speech of burning wrath and almost fabulous lengths against the Liberal candidate and his party. That party has committed a deadly sin against the priests in sympathising with Italy - in wishing to see the Italians obtain that liberty and independence which Roman Catholics of this country long struggled by the side of the English Liberals to obtain for themselves, and which, when they have obtained it, they would ungenerously deny to their poor downtrodden co-religionists in Italy. Mr Brassey would not sacrifice his noble feeling of sympathy with the Italian race, and therefore the priests resolved to sacrifice him. They knew that Lord Derby had spoken in favour of Italian dismemberment and the maintenance of the temporal power of the Pope, and, knowing the parties are now nearly balanced in the House of Commons, and that the Conservative leader is again looking forward to office, they resolved to seize the opportunity of strengthening of the ranks of Toryism in Parliament. They saw that the

---

[78] Cheshire Observer, 11th Dec, 1861

> Liberal party was divided; they were aware that the contest, without them, would be close and severe; and they resolved to throw their whole flock into the scale of Laird and Derbyism, and thus bring it down with a triumphant shock. and the priests have succeeded in their project.[79]

Admittedly, Chapman was doing no more than M'Neile had been doing in Liverpool for the previous twenty years and more. But the manner of his processing his flock to the polls, caused great offence. In 1861 voting was still done openly. The voter publicly committed to one candidate or another. Canon Chapman decided that the voters he had persuaded would all arrive together. This gave, rightly or wrongly, the impression that he was herding them. The Liverpool Mercury reported:

> BIRKENHEAD ELECTION: THE POLLING
>
> At eight o'clock, yesterday morning, the polling for the borough commenced. At the opening of the booths there was a rush on the part of the friends of both the candidates to secure the first place. Up to half past nine o'clock, Mr Brassey headed the poll by a majority of fifty; at this hour the very Reverend Canon Chapman, leading some three hundred and fourteen Catholic voters, appeared. The very Rev. gentleman was accompanied by Mr F. O'Byrne and others. The appearance of Canon Chapman was hailed with shouts of acclamation by the friends of Mr Laird, who speedily formed a passage for them to the polling booth. Canon Chapman first went forward, and registered his vote for Mr Laird, and the Catholics forming the procession went in succession and followed his example. During the time thus occupied the cheering and huzzas which rent the air could be heard in remote districts of the town. It was all through the contest anticipated, and it has so

[79] Liverpool Mercury, 11th Dec, 1861

> turned out, for from the time the Catholics voted until the close of the poll. Mr Laird kept the lead by a majority varying from 289 to 306 until the close when the majority ascertained was stated to be 323.[80]

John Laird secured victory by 1661 votes to 1338, according to the Liverpool Mercury. The Cheshire Observer however gave the votes as 1643 for Mr Laird and 1296 for Mr Brassey; a majority of 347. This seems to be the figure that became the public memory. He spoke to a crowd estimated at 12,000 from the balcony of his house in Hamilton Square, as did a number of his campaign team, among whom was Canon Chapman:

> Brother electors, I come forward to congratulate you upon the great victory which we have won this day (cheers). You have fought the good fight, and you have gained a great cause. You have by your votes declared that the man who I, as a minister of religion, last Saturday declared to be great in his charities - you have declared that man to be a fitting member to represent the working men of Birkenhead (cheers), and the interests of Birkenhead (cheers). You have declared him truly (uproar) - you have declared him truly to be the father of the poor of Birkenhead (loud cheers). Go home to your own firesides and tell your families how you have worked and laboured this day, and what a great victory you have won. Goodnight, and when we meet again for such a contest may it be carried on with such good humour, such sobriety and such temperance as may become the electors and men of Birkenhead (cheers).[81]

That speech represented Canon Chapman in his pomp. In his arrogance in dragooning his parishioners he had put John Laird in an impossible position. Laird's core constituency was Orange bigots.

---

[80] Liverpool Daily Post, 10th Dec, 1861

[81] Cheshire Observer, 14th Dec, 1861

There couldn't be an accommodation between people who thought the Pope was the Antichrist and those who thought he was infallible: between those who believed the Bible was the word of God, the literal truth, and those who believed the Catholic church was the guide to faith and morals. In practical terms Canon Chapman had very publicly made it appear that Laird was in his debt. The Liverpool Mercury commented:

> Placed between the two stools of popery and no-popery, the Tory member for Birkenhead will certainly fall to the ground unless he ... have sufficient courage to release himself from that unenviable position by discarding the claims of one of his two allies. Sooner or later Mr Laird must do so; and the rejected suitor will not be Mr Knox.[82]

The Cheshire Observer ran a headline:

> WHO DID IT? WHO DID IT? WHY CANON CHAPMAN OF COURSE.
>
> The election is now over; but its moral and social results will remain for some time. ... There is no doubt that coercion of a very repulsive and unconstitutional character was resorted to by Canon Chapman over the Catholic electors; and little doubt exists that the subserviency of hundreds of that class to the will of one man, is a fact that will not and ought not to be soon forgotten.[83]

In another article the same, Liberal newspaper reported:

> Soon after the first return was issued, the Reverend Canon Chapman, with one or two other Catholic priests of the District, headed between two and three hundred of their flocks - what a good shepherd to

---

[82] Ibid

[83] Ibid

> guide his lambs in things political as well as spiritual - march to the polling booths. It is not unreasonable to assume, from what has come to our knowledge, that his followers had assembled that morning at early mass, had been exhorted, and, in fact, compelled and coerced by the Very Rev Canon and his coadjutors, and others, to follow the very Rev. gentleman to the poll, and record their votes for the Tory candidate. In times long past, when good old George the Third was King, and the Tories ruled the roost, we have heard of ancient aristocratic Tory landowners driving up their tenants to the poll, like so many sheep to the slaughterhouse, to vote for a certain candidate. In those days a Catholic priest in England had not the privilege. But modern reforms have given the power; and the Reverend Canon Chapman, it would seem, was in no way scrupulous in its exercise. What unenviable notoriety the very Rev. gentleman has gained? Over and over again it was alleged, before the emancipation of the Catholics, by the old and invested and inveterate Tories, that the Catholics were not fit to be entrusted with the franchise, because they must, for fear of excommunication, vote as the priest dictated. This was denied. But in the procedure at this election, the fact has been powerfully and incontestably demonstrated, for we find the Reverend Canon Chapman not only voting himself for the party, who from time to time immemorial, strenuously offered every opposition to the church to which he belongs, but compelling, by intimidation, his flock to follow his example.[84]

The hostility of conservatives to Canon Chapman was made apparent in February 1862. A banquet was held in honour of John Laird at Birkenhead music hall. Leading Laird supporters spoke in his favour,

---

[84] Ibid

Mr Derbyshire, a Birkenhead magistrate, rose to speak to the audience, including Canon Chapman. The audience had been led to expect him to propose a vote of thanks to Cannon Chapman. Their reaction showed they were not prepared to listen to any such thing:

> Mr Derbyshire then rose, amidst some applause and a few cries of "sit down", to address the company. After a few preliminary remarks, he said that stigmas had been cast on a certain portion of the community for voting for Mr Laird.[85]

This was an obvious reference to Canon Chapman and the Catholic voters for Laird:

> He (Mr Derbyshire) never asked any person for a vote, but he said they were greatly indebted, and he could not be charged with anything like courting the favour of any individual present - (hisses and uproar) - for he might be considered an ultra-Protestant - ("hear, hear" and hisses) - but he might say that but for the manner in which the Roman Catholic clergy of Birkenhead conducted themselves, they might have had a serious row. (Laughter, applause, and groans.)[86]

It was now clear to Mr Derbyshire that his audience would never agree to a vote of thanks. He was floundering, trying to find a basic minimum in which his audience might agree. His prepared speech was a non-starter:

> They did all in their power to prevent intoxication and therefore those gentlemen (the Catholic clergy), deserved, he considered their best thanks - (hisses and great uproar) - for being, as it were, the

85 Liverpool Mercury, 5th February, 1862

86 Ibid

> guardians of the peace.
>
> They exerted the power which they had in their hands for the good of the day and to prevent intoxication. (Renewed hisses and other expressions of disapprobation, during which the speaker could not proceed for further, booing, heckling and jeering.)[87]

Mr Derbyshire abandoned his speech. It was plainly apparent that there was nothing, nothing at all, that anyone, even a close ally of John Laird, could say in favour of Catholic priests, and Canon Chapman in particular, to a Conservative audience. They could not even be thanked for preventing another "Irish row", as the rowdy behaviour of Irish crowds was then commonly referred.

John Laird rose to address the 347 guests. 347 had been the size of his majority and about the number of Catholic voters that Canon Chapman had persuaded to vote for him:

> Mr Laird, on rising to respond to the toast, was enthusiastically cheered. He returned his best thanks to the canvassers who had worked so hard on his behalf, and returned him by so large a majority as 347 - and by an extraordinary coincidence he was told by a memorandum which had just been sent to him, that they in that room sitting at dinner numbered 347. His opponents had objected to his return because he was supported by men of all parties - because churchmen, Roman Catholics, Orangemen and dissenters all supported him. However, now the election was over, he might repeat what he said at the close of the election, that he would consider himself a member for every person, in that borough, to do the best he could to promote their interests, whether they opposed him or whether they supported him.[88]

---

87 Ibid

88 Ibid

John Laird was making it very clear that he acknowledged no debt to Canon Chapman and would not act in the interests of the Catholic Church or the Pope. On all sides the knives were out for Canon Chapman and the Catholics of Birkenhead. It is only in this context that Birkenhead's Garibaldi riots can be understood. Chapman's opponents, and there were many of them, were looking for any excuse to pin the blame for bad Irish Catholic behaviour on him. For the likes of Dr Baylee and A Looker On both Canon Chapman and Catholics in general had to be restored to their proper place - the Outer Darkness.

CHAPTER SEVEN

Birkenhead Garibaldi Riots

In October 1862 the Rev Baylee engineered an episode of public disorder, for which the Catholics were blamed. Further, he and other clerics used the reaction to disorder, to pressure the authorities into an attack on the Catholics of the North End. He also conspired to bring militants of the Orange Order to Birkenhead. It seemed that the only person alert to his manipulation was Sir Edward Cust, Chairman of the Birkenhead magistrates. Ironically, The Times and several Liverpool newspapers sought to blame Cust himself for his supposed cowardice in not violently suppressing disorder.

The autumn of 1862 was a time of crisis for the papacy, which in turn brought about a moral panic in Great Britain, and an opportunity for anti-Catholic conspiracy theorists. Garibaldi, the leading Italian Nationalist, and man of action, had decided the time had come to take up arms against the Papal States. Armies under his command had already liberated much of Italy. Garibaldi was regarded as a hero by liberals in Europe and the Americas.

The Papal States of Italy[89]

Garibaldi's liberation of Naples in 1860:

ODE TO GARIBALDI

ON THE MORNING OF THE 7TH NOVEMBER 1860, WHEN HE ENTERED THE CITY OF NAPLES, SEATED BY THE SIDE OF KING VICTOR EMMANUEL, AMID THE ENTHUSIASTIC SHOUTS OF A LIBERATED PEOPLE.

Awake! arise! Parthenope!
In all thy borders sing;

[89] westerncivguidesumwblogs.org/2013/11/11/italianunification-4, accessed 2/11/20

The Liberator brings to thee
Thy chosen King:
Himself first to proclaim
The glorious name,
Hail! King of Italy!
Yes! mark that well!
'Twas the Dictator's voice
Announc'd thy choice;
Let not Remembrance fail!
In this most holy cause,
Nations around who dwell,
The joyous sound shall swell,
With glad applause,
And Italy rejoice in all her homes;
He comes! He comes!
Hail! Victor! Hail! Victor Emmanuel!
'Twas Garibaldi led the way
On to this glorious day;
He the great battle won,
In almost hopeless hour
With more than mortal power
He spoke and it was done.
Hail! Garibaldi! Hail!
Who stayed Italia's wail;
Blessed forever be this happy morn;
So dost the eternal gratitude entail
On millions yet unborn.
Victor is King of Italy - but Thou
Art King of men, by grace divine,

Drawing their hearts to thine:
By Poet - prophet erst foretold,
As in the days of old,
On earth should come, and how;
For by the Florentine had been,
In mental vision seen
What we all witness now:
Thine was the hand that struck
The foul oppressor down,
And from his pallid brow,
In righteousness to pluck
A blood-stained crown.
Duke Garibaldi came,
As one set forth from God,
Angel of Justice and of right,
And with an everlasting rod
Of pow'r and might
His enemies, afraid, did tremble at his name,
To them consuming flame,
But to his own, by fervent valour fed,
Patriots ambitious of a soldier's bed,
It had a power to charm,
As from all harm,
And made them love to follow where he led,
Good wise, and brave,
To ev'ry true-born son,
And made Italia's children feel as one.
His heart was strong to save,
His mind to plan, and so the God-like man,

By land and sea,
With works and words made Italy to be
A name no longer, but a Kingdom free
So all not yet done - since there remains
Venetia writhing in remorseless chains,
And the she-wolf upon the Tiber reigns.[90]

The 'she-wolf on the Tiber' was the Catholic Church. Liberal attitudes to the papacy and to the government of Rome and the Papal States were hostile. The Mercury printed the following on papal government:

> THE PAPAL GOVERNMENT AND THE PAPAL POLICE
>
> ... The police of the Roman government are already well-known to be all that the police of a government must be when that government has no laws. The principle of such a government is arbitrary power because its head, according to his own belief, derives his authority directly from God. Nor is any distinction between the temporal and spiritual sphere recognised; when he wishes anything, God wishes it. The authority of these subaltern agents is an emanation of his arbitrary power, not subject to superior control, as if what emanates from God could be in direct contradiction with the eternal principles of justice and of natural right. The higher clergy verse receive carte blanche from Heaven; The spies and informers receive the same from the government; their subjects must submit in silence - nay, if they wish to be honest and loyal, according to the standards of honesty and loyalty of their rulers, they ought to bless the hand of the most abject member of society at the very moment of its smiting them,

[90] Liverpool Mercury, November 24th, 1860

> because it smites them in the name of the priests, and the priests govern in the name of God. This is the spirit which animates the rotten machine of clerical government - a government with so many foreign hirelings who would support and avenge by spilling the blood of the poor Romans, whose countless wounds these foreign hirelings are either, in their stupidity, unable to perceive, or, in their hypocrisy, unwilling to acknowledge. Viewing this form of government from a distance, they have believed it to be religious and Christian; had they contemplated it more closely, they would not for a single moment have hesitated to recognise it as pure Paganism.[91]

In the past the Mercury had tended to be sympathetic to Catholic causes in Birkenhead, but when it came to criticism of Garibaldi, the Mercury was as unsympathetic to Catholic grievances as Conservative newspapers.

---

91 Liverpool Mercury, June 16th, 1860

Garibaldi entering Naples in Triumph with the King of Italy[92]

In October 1862 Garibaldi recruited a new volunteer army and marched against the Pope, very much against the advice of the new King of Italy. The Papal States were defended by the army of France then Europe's leading military power. Garibaldi was intercepted by an Italian army, wounded, and imprisoned. Liberals in Europe were appalled by his treatment. Speakers in Hyde Park spoke in his favour. Those speakers were attacked and displaced by Irishmen, who were, in turn, attacked by off-duty soldiers. These disturbances became known as Garibaldi Riots. There was a moral panic, led by The Times newspaper, about Irish mobs denying English rights to free speech across the country.

In September 1862, Father Gavazzi visited Tralee. He was a former papal official who had converted to Protestantism and made a good living delivering antipapal rants. He had been responsible for rioting and deaths in Canada where he had made a speaking tour. Five died when troops shot at a crowd of rioting Irishmen.

The good Protestants of Tralee ... chose to invite

92 Illustrated London News, September 22nd, 1860

> Father Gavazzi to hold forth in the city against the Pope and the papacy. Gavazzi has held forth many hundreds of thousands of times in this metropolis to admiring and sympathetic audiences. The people want to hear Rome well abused, and they've heard it. ... To take him to Tralee seems to us as much the same sort of thing as if one took the burning coals out of the fire and spread them among the clothes in the laundry, or discharged a Congreve rocket down Cheapside. Of course Gavazzi, while perfectly harmless in the London concert-room, would set Tralee on fire. He did, and at this moment the few Protestants in Tralee no longer live in glass houses. Glazed windows are a luxury, which can only be enjoyed with the goodwill of the populace. They are hostages to your goodwill to that susceptible personage.[93]

What the leader writer of The Times was saying, was that people who went into Irish Catholic spaces should be respectful of Irish Catholics. If they were not, then there would be consequences. The consequences were often smashed windows, a popular form of Irish protest. The Times was well aware of Catholic Irish feelings on Garibaldi and the consequences of inflaming Irish sentiments, as must Baylee have been. It seems that within the British Empire, and Ireland was still thought of as part of the empire, not as the home country, the religious susceptibilities of the natives had to be considered. In Ireland, there were laws to prevent Orangemen from provoking their Catholic neighbours. Unfortunately, there was little awareness that such laws might need to apply in England where Catholic Irishmen had moved in their hundreds of thousands, along with militant Orange vicars in the Church of England.

In October 1862, Father Gavazzi arrived in Liverpool where he had been booked to give a series of lectures. The authorities were aware of the threat to public order he represented. There were no spare policemen in Liverpool; outbreaks of sectarian disorder were

[93] The Times, 30th September, 1862

anticipated.

Dr Baylee's church, Holy Trinity, was situated in Birkenhead's North End. By 1862 it was estimated that it was surrounded by over 10,000 Catholic Irish who had been attracted by relatively well paid, unskilled labour in the building of the new docks. It was now an Irish Catholic space. Holy Trinity Church in Price Street was built in what had been a Protestant area; it was a Protestant area no longer.

Attached to the church was an annexe which was used by the Birkenhead Parliamentary Debating Society. This was an organisation set up by Dr Baylee to give training in public speaking to some of his congregation. The topic for debate on 8th October 1862, was 'Garibaldi and Italy'. Garibaldi had just been wounded and captured by papal forces. Two days before the debate, placards appeared in the windows of the annexe, saying "Sympathy for Garibaldi." The placards were coloured orange. It was never established who placed the placards, but Dr Baylee would be by far the most likely candidate. He had had over 40 years of experience antagonising people, by displaying placards usually orange in colour. They were designed to enrage the population; had they been placed in a window in Ireland it would have been a criminal offence.

The local population duly became enraged. There had been stories of an impending 'row' circulating throughout the day. The Society was in session, and a service was being held in the church when a large and noisy crowd gathered outside and broke the windows. The local police were already on hand; they had been warned. Canon Chapman must also have been aware and made sure he was well away from the town. Part of Baylee's plan was to discredit him further.

The police were reluctant to intervene but stood ready to protect local shops. Dr Baylee's son, also a Rev. Baylee, went to the church house of St Werburgh's, where he found the curate, Father Brundit. Father Brundit went to Holy Trinity Church, and addressed the crowd, asking them to disperse, which eventually they did.

Police tactics, in not confronting the rioters, were justified, according to the early accounts:

> It required the greatest discretion on his part, to prevent a collision between his men and the rioters - a collision from which the police, from the paucity of

> their number, must surely have been worsted. ... Fortunately, the Reverend Father Brundit, and the Reverend Father Golding (Catholic priests) made their appearance in Price Street about eight o'clock. After remonstrating with the mob on the impropriety of their conduct, the reverend gentlemen succeeded in persuading the greater portion of them to disperse. The priests were lustily cheered and were followed by the rioters to the North End.[94]

In this narrative, the contribution of the Catholic clergy was a positive one and is consistent with the events being just 'another Irish row', in which the possibilities of harm and injury had been averted by restrained policing and clerical intervention. A Mercury report shortly after the riot started, appeared to minimise its impact:

> THE GARIBALDIAN RIOT AT BIRKENHEAD
>
> Yesterday, some glaziers were employed in repairing the damage done to the windows of Holy Trinity Church and the Institute at the back, by the mob of Irish Roman Catholics who assembled to prevent the Parliamentary Debating Society expressing their sympathy with Garibaldi and Italy, on Wednesday evening. The damage done to the sacred edifice has been considerable, but perhaps not so serious as was at first anticipated. A quantity of stones, broken ware, and other missiles was removed from the church by the women who were engaged to clean the place. Since the night of the riot no further attempt has been made to commit a breach of the peace. It seems that the ruffians, in addition to attacking Holy Trinity Church and the Institute, broke a number of panes of glass in the windows of the small Welsh Baptist Chapel, in Price Street, and some glass was also broken in Saint Paul's United Presbyterian Church, Jackson Street, Grange Lane.

[94] Ibid

> The latter building is situated a considerable distance from Price Street, where the disturbance commenced, and it is therefore supposed that the damage at this place of worship was committed by some of the rioters on their way home. Much regret is expressed in the township that the ringleaders were not captured, so that the magistrates might have had an opportunity of punishing them by a heavy sentence of imprisonment, and thus striking terror among a set of ruffians who would set law and order at defiance.
>
> At the usual meeting of the magistrates yesterday morning, the Rev. Dr Baylee, incumbent of Holy Trinity Church (who was accompanied by his son, the Rev. Joseph Baylee) attended, and in the course of some remarks said he thought it rather strange that no arrest had been made, Having stated that he did not complain of the conduct of the police he said that his son had been struck on the hat with a stone, and he wished to know who was to pay for the damage done to his church and the institute. Edward Cust said the bench were very sorry no person had been apprehended. If any of the rioters were, information might be laid against them; and if they were convicted, then the damage done to property would have to be made good at the expense of the Hundred of Wirral. In leaving the cause, the Reverend Dr Baylee was understood to say that it was the intention of those connected with him to hold another meeting, as they were determined not to be put down by brute force.[95]

It would require some effort to transform the narrative into one in which Catholic priests were responsible for a riot, but Baylee and others quickly set about it.

Dr Baylee called what the Liverpool Daily Post described as an "Indignation Meeting." It was at this meeting, held on 13th October,

---

[95] Liverpool Mercury, October 10th, 1862

that Baylee succeeded in reframing the events of the previous week:

> THE LATE ROMAN CATHOLIC RIOT AT BIRKENHEAD
>
> Last evening, a crowded meeting of influential gentlemen connected with the township of Birkenhead and the neighbourhood (called by circular issued by the Rev. Dr Baylee), took place at the Park Hotel, to consider what steps should be taken in consequence of the attack made on Wednesday night last, upon Holy Trinity Church and the institute connected therewith, by a mob of Irish Roman Catholics.
>
> Present at the meeting was Dr Baylee and his son Rev Joseph Baylee, five other Protestant vicars, John and William Laird, Mr Hind, chairman of the Birkenhead Improvement Commission, Mr Wain, law clerk to the Commission and a number of other leading citizens. Dr Baylee was called to address for the meeting:
>
> The Rev. Dr Baylee then explained to the meeting that for a considerable time there had been in connection with this church a useful working men's college. In conjunction with that college was a debating society, which met once a fortnight, and discussed nothing but politics - religious subjects being excluded. The subject to be discussed last Wednesday night was "Garibaldi and Italy". Until the placards were out, he knew nothing about the subject that was to be debated, for he left the conduct of the debates to the members themselves. There was nothing offensive in the notice calling the meeting, for not a word was said about the Pope.[96]

He expected his audience to believe that he, who was notorious for posting orange-coloured placards, knew nothing about

96 Liverpool Mercury, 14th October, 1862

orange-coloured placards. He also expected them to believe that the papacy, under attack from Garibaldi and his allies, was not an issue that Catholics might be sensitive about.

> An intimation having been given that the Roman Catholics of the township would not allow the meeting to take place, some person went to the police office at two o'clock, or certainly not later than four, to inform the police that the meeting was likely to be interrupted. The Reverend gentleman then detailed at some length the nature of the attack which had been made upon the Institute and Holy Trinity Church, which resulted in the Parliamentary Debating Society not attempting to hold the meeting, and the service in the church being abruptly brought to a close by the mob who had assembled, having broken the windows of both buildings. The police were present, and yet not a single arrest was made. For an hour and a half, the township was in the hands of an unsuppressed mob, who also broke some windows in a Welsh church and the United Presbyterian Church in Jackson Street.[97]

It is worth pointing out that if the mob were genuinely 'unsuppressed', a number of things might be expected to happen. People leaving the church or the institute might be attacked, the mob might be expected to leave the Irish area of town or other things than windows might be attacked. None of those things happened. The violence, such as it was, was limited and targeted.

Having stated that he waited on the following day upon the magistrates, but obtained no satisfaction, the Reverend gentleman said he now gave notice that he would not submit as an English subject to have his civil rights taken away, and that he expected the magistrates to protect them (applause). … He then read the following letter which he had received from a gentleman of respectability in the township, respecting the recent riot:

---

97 Ibid

TO THE CHAIRMAN

Birkenhead, Oct 18, 1862

Sir, - I wish to make a statement which may be of some interest to the meeting. When the mob left Holy Trinity Church, they followed the priest into Watson Street, where he addressed them. I distinctly heard the following in his speech: "I find no fault with what you have done tonight. For my own part, I consider Garibaldi a Viper, a blackguard: I can call him nothing else, because of his doings in our beloved Italy. And therefore, as true Catholics, it is our duty to be against him, or against any movement which tends to sympathise with him. Garibaldi demands not the slightest sympathy from us. (Several voices: 'Hear, hear'.) You have prevented their having a meeting, because they were compelled to put out the gas and close the doors. Thus, you have gained a glorious victory - (loud applause, and a voice: 'Three cheers for the Pope,' followed by deafening cheers) - and all of you consider it as a victory; and now go home to your own fireside, and then talk it over with your wives and children." At this I left them, and proceeded down Watson Street, during which time I heard the voice of the priest still addressing them, but I could not tell what he said. I then stopped in Beckwith Street and watched the whole proceedings. The people seemed very much infuriated, and loud and thrilling cries of "Three cheers for the Pope" rent the air. At length I perceived two priests coming down Beckwith Street alone. I watched them until out of sight, and then proceeded homewards.

N.B. - I certify that the above statements are correct and challenge contradiction. I certify to the credibility of the person who addressed this letter to me to be placed in the hands of the chairman. - Your obedient

> servant, Joseph Baylee[98]

So this was the evidence of priestly connivance the meeting was invited to consider: an anonymous letter from an English gentleman walking through the Irish quarter of town, blithely unconcerned by 'unsuppressed' mob violence.

> Mr W. Hind (Chairman of the Commissioners) who was called upon by the chairman, said it appeared to him that the question was one that ought to be approached with great moderation and forbearance. He referred to the recent riots in Ireland and in the metropolis, and that connected with the magic name of Garibaldi there was joined the downfall of popery.[99]

It was clearly obvious to Mr Hind, that any discussion of Garibaldi was going to be a sensitive issue to Catholics in 1862. He was aware of such sensitivities, as others ought to have been.

> The Birkenhead Parliamentary Debating Society, he did not deny, had a perfect right to discuss any subject they thought proper, but he suggested whether they would not have acted with more discretion had they chosen another time, seeing the excitement that existed in the public mind. Having referred to the conduct of the police, which he admitted was a fair matter for inquiry, he moved "that it is not desirable that any public meeting should be called to ascertain facts which could be in a more desirable form ascertained by other proceedings." If they were prepared to hold a public meeting, he contended that they should be prepared to pay a portion of the responsibility and not to throw the whole of it upon the authorities, who had only

[98] Ibid

[99] Ibid

> limited means at their disposal; the police force only amounting to 55.[100]

The clear advice from the chairman of the Improvement Commission was that anybody could have predicted that holding that debate, in that place, at that time was asking for trouble. He further urged that holding another debate on the same subject, in that place, in the future would bring further disturbances.

> Mr Sloman seconded the motion, and in doing so urged that a public meeting would be attended with danger to all concerned.[101]

In the 19th century, a gathering of three or more people to carry out a common purpose, whether lawful or unlawful, in such circumstances as would in the opinion of firm and rational men, endanger the public peace or create fear of immediate danger to the tranquillity of the neighbourhood, was an unlawful assembly. Both Mr Hind and Mr Sloman had expressly warned Dr Baylee that what he was proposing would create danger to the tranquillity of the North End and of Birkenhead. They were firm and rational men. What was his response?

> A long discussion followed, in which Dr Baylee expressed his intention, whatever resolution might be adopted, to hold the meeting of the Parliamentary Debating Society on Wednesday night next.[102]

So much for the complete independence of the Society to select the topics for discussion. What emerged from the meeting was a proposal from the proponents of Law and Order, and the authorities responsible for it, to do something which was illegal. What was proposed should have been quashed by the Cheshire Magistrates, instead, to a large extent, they colluded with it.

The last thing that John Laird and the Commissioners could afford

---

100 Ibid

101 Ibid

102 Ibid

was Protestant martyrs. Laird especially was sensitive to any charge that he was protecting Catholics. Rumours were still circulating as late as 1865 about a supposed deal between him and Canon Chapman as a return for Catholic support at the 1861 election. The magistrates began to prepare, to call in reinforcements for the police from the Cheshire Constabulary, calling and swearing-in several thousand special constables and summoning armed soldiers from Manchester.

Meanwhile, Father Brundrit attempted to deal with Baylee's accusations, he wrote to the Mercury:

> GENTLEMEN - In the Mercury of this day I find an account of a meeting held respecting the late riot in Birkenhead. At that meeting was read a letter containing an imaginary speech by me. As usual in such cases the writer does not give his name; but a certain Joseph Baylee vouches he is a credible and respectable person. Perhaps he is the same very respectable and very credible person who has set it abroad that he saw Canon Chapman (who was more than 50 miles from Birkenhead at the time) inciting the crowd to break the windows. Whoever this anonymous calumniator may be, I unhesitatingly state that no such speech was made by me, nor by Father Golden, nor by any other priest, and the writer of the letter must indeed have long ears to have heard what was never uttered. I did tell the people to go home, and I did call Garibaldi a blackguard. I may have called him a viper, though I do not think I did. It is a name which is more applicable to that ungrateful man, who rushed to the priests to seek their aid to save his windows and slandered them afterwards, because at personal risk and inconvenience, they had saved the town from riots and bloodshed. Though repudiating the speech put into my mouth I wish it to be perfectly understood that I do not by any means lay the blame of this row on the Catholics.
>
> I did not even know that this famous meeting of a debating society was going to be held until the Rev.

J.T. Baylee, son of Dr Baylee, arrived at St Werburgh's priests' house, and begged me to go to the scene of the commotion and try to quell it. At great inconvenience to myself, I left the class I was instructing and hurried to Trinity Church, where I used my utmost endeavours to quiet the justly excited Catholics, and succeeded, with Father Golden, in dispersing them and preventing further destruction of property.

If misguided fanatics choose to call a meeting by large, orange-coloured placards headed "Sympathy for Garibaldi," in the very centre of 15,000 Catholics, they must take the consequences and be answerable for them. They say they will hold another meeting. Let them do as they like. I promise them in the name of myself and my colleagues that we will not again act policemen, but those who raise the storm may allay it.

ROBERT WRIGHT BRUNDRIT, M. A.

St, Werburg's, Birkenhead, Oct. 14, 1862[103]

Brundrit was well aware that Baylee wished to implicate Canon Chapman. Chapman was a charismatic and forceful character with undoubted influence over his parishioners, as the previous year's election had shown. Even his Catholic parishioners had complained of his anti-Garibaldi tirades. He was the prime candidate for demagogue. His diplomatic absence from Birkenhead was most fortunate. Baylee had had to settle for Brundrit, now Brundrit was making it very clear that he did not want the role of demagogue either.

The next day, organised Protestantism began to march. The arguments put forward by Baylee were to be tested on the streets of Birkenhead. The Birkenhead authorities had committed themselves to the story that 'free speech' was threatened by low Irish Catholics, led by their priests, and they had to be taught a lesson. Baylee and his associates had succeeded in taking over the intellectual space in which policy was decided.

---

103 Liverpool Mercury, 15th October, 1862

The Birkenhead authorities began by recruiting ratepayers as special constables. According to newspaper reports, as many as 3,000 were sworn in, given staves, and asked to report for duty on Wednesday, October 15th. A substantial proportion of the Birkenhead Protestant population had volunteered. It could not be often in a Birkenhead Protestant man's life that an opportunity arose to break Irish Catholic heads, encouraged by the knowledge of a righteous cause, and sanctioned by the local MP and employer, magistrates, vicars and neighbours. The opportunity was taken up with alacrity.

On 14th October a 'Protestant Demonstration' was held at Hope Hall in Liverpool. Rev Dr Blakeney, vicar of Christ Church, Claughton, then just outside Birkenhead and yet another Irish Evangelical, addressed the largely Orange audience:

> A great demonstration in defence of Protestantism and Orangeism, intended as a counterblast to the popish aggressions and outrages which have recently taken place in various parts of the country, was held last night in the Hope Hall, Hope Street. The spacious room was filled to overflowing, the audience consisting chiefly of men of the working classes; every seat was occupied, while, notwithstanding this crush, many people were unable to obtain admission. The proceedings were of the most enthusiastic character, but were orderly and, no attempt being made to interrupt the harmony of the proceedings.
>
> ... The Rev. Dr Blakeney said, they were accustomed to boast of the civil and religious liberties they enjoyed in this country, and they had indeed reason to thank God for the great blessings and privileges they enjoyed; but now it must be manifest to the most obtuse in intellect and observation that there were those in this country who are labouring to deprive them of their civil and religious liberties. (Hear, hear.)
>
> ... And let it not be supposed that this was a mere Irish movement, that it was to be attributed to Irishmen and their love of disturbance. That was far

from the case. He believed there was no man fonder of fair play and more attached to it than Paddy himself; but Paddy in these instances was made to bear a blame which did not really attach to him. The blame was not to be laid at the door of Irishmen as Irishmen, but it was to be laid at the door of the church of Rome.

... In truth, Romanism was an intolerant power, and if it prevailed in this country, it would trample our civil and religious liberties in the very dust. (Cheers) A friend asked what would result from the movement if Roman Catholics succeeded in the steps they were now taking to put down freedom of speech and discussion. He had no doubt of what would take place. If popery in its various forms on the one hand, and democracy in its various forms on the other hand, if superstition and rationalism were permitted, he was persuaded they would succeed in introducing anarchy, confusion, and disorder (cheers) - and the glorious fabric of our constitution, which was cemented by the blood of the martyred forefathers, would fade away like a morning cloud. (Cries of "Never".) He joined in the cry, but it was not by saying "Never", that they would succeed in their efforts. They must follow up the cry by deeds - they must follow up their profession by exertions, and by the exertions they must throw back the tide of popery and rationalism, roll back those assailants and stand in the breach in the defence of our glorious liberties in church and state (applause). They must stand on the old constitution which was inaugurated by the Revolution of 1688 (cheers). They must maintain the principles that placed William of Orange on the throne (renewed cheers). They must hand down those principles and those privileges to their children and to their children's children. If they had a long pull, and a strong pull, and they pull together, then, by the grace and the blessing of God, the result to

> which he had referred would never, never take place (applause).[104]

This was the language of militant Irish Protestantism being used to fire up Orangemen to attack Irish Catholics in Birkenhead. The lead role in promoting violence was taken by Birkenhead's Orange clergymen. Some 300 Liverpool Orangemen arrived in Birkenhead on the evening of 15th October ready to fight.

In addition to the special constables, Captain William Laird led 300 volunteers from the shipyard, there were workmen from Brassey's Canada Works, the Cheshire Rifle Volunteers and 175 men of the 49th Foot. All of these were reinforcements for a police presence, the full Birkenhead complement of about 60, and 20 to 50, according to different reports, of the Cheshire Constabulary. There was simply no prospect of a successful anti-Garibaldi action.

The most Insightful account of the events of the 15th of October is to be found in the Dublin-based Catholic Telegraph. Unlike the overwhelmingly anti-Irish and anti-priest accounts to be found in the English press, it did not rely on Birkenhead police briefings.

> The local authorities being duly informed - by the Garibaldians of course - that an emeute (a riot) would in all probability take place, some measures were taken to suppress it, should it occur, instead of preventing it all together. But the most remarkable feature in the proceedings is that all the forces called in were known to be as favourable to the side of the debaters and their followers, as they were rancorously hostile to the Irish who constituted the opposite party. First among this motley array there were 60 of the borough police, 20 of the county constabulary, 1000 special constables, 175 of the military; and to show the true colours of the party that were to be supported and let loose upon the "Irishry", three hundred members of the Orange Society.

[104] Liverpool Courier, 15th October, 1862

... Everyone on this side of the Channel knows what a sensation would be caused among the Catholic population of a locality if 300 Orangemen, with a large body of police and military, 1000 special constables, and a considerable portion of the Protestant inhabitants, armed with formidable bludgeons, politely designated heavy batons, to aid them, were seen marching through the streets in 'fours'. The cry at so formidable an array would most probably be, 'Aux armes citoyens', as in the days of the French Revolution. What gentle means this posse of Garibaldian heroes took, to preserve peace and order, may be learnt from the following account of the glorious exploit, performed by a body of these peace preservers. This account, be it especially remembered, is given by the Liverpool Mercury, a journal of strong Garibaldian sympathies, and runs thus:

'At the corner of Cathcart Street and Price Street, a scene occurred which reflected discredit on the police. A body of some 20 police officers marched along the footpath down Cathcart Street, and as they turned into Price Street a young man was quietly leaning against the palings fronting the houses, making no noise, having no companions, and apparently taking no part in the noisy proceedings near the church, when the police struck him down in the most violent manner. The poor fellow fell senseless to the ground, but the police proceeded without at all troubling their minds as to the consequences of their most reprehensible conduct. The inhabitants of the neighbouring houses who witnessed the affair say that the man was struck twice by the police; and those who surrounded him immediately afterwards declared that he was killed. For the truth of either of these statements we cannot vouch, but our own observation enables us to assert most positively that the man was struck by the police;

that he fell, as we have said senseless to the ground; and that, when raised, the blood flowed freely from his mouth and nose. Though not then dead he was quite powerless, and beyond all question he sustained injury of a very serious character. We may add that the spot where this took place was a considerable distance from the church, as all was quiet when the police came up, and there was nothing whatever to call for such brutal conduct on their part."

No, so after this specimen of the mildness and forbearance shown by the guardians of the peace, paid by Catholics as well as Protestants - by Irishmen as well as Englishmen - we asked whether it is consistent with the impartiality which ought to distinguish the comments of the press, that the leading journal of the Empire should offer no remark whatever on such savages and such savagery, whilst it designates the Irish, "Popish ruffians," an "Irish mob and their priestly instigators," an "organised gang of ruffians," etc? Is it that before the trial of the Irishmen who were arrested on the occasion - once the case is still sub judice - The Times or any other journal should urge the government to "punish them with the utmost severity - that an example should be made of the miscreants (the Irish, of course) who were concerned in the disturbance"? Not a word about the originators of it - all the writer's ingenuity is exercised in endeavouring to show that the attack was " a premeditated one, organised for days before by the Roman Catholics."

Not a syllable touching the provocations, the rumours, and whisperings that a disciplined, armed, and overwhelming force would, once and for all, put down the Catholics of the borough and its vicinity - not a single allusion to all this is made in the Times' account of the affray; it begs the question by saying, that the object of the Irish was "to show to the people of Birkenhead that they were strong enough to prevent any expression of opinion adverse to themselves in the new borough". So far as we are concerned, we should be the first to condemn any suppression of individual or public opinion, but there may be circumstances connected with such an expression of opinion that would very much change the nature of the case. It might be out of season - it might be expressed for the sole purpose of insulting and exciting a considerable portion of the community - and, in the latter case, it could not be strictly considered an expression of public opinion. Lastly, it might have been expressed solely for the purpose of affording a plea and pretext to the stronger party to attack a weaker, and that the weaker party whose feelings and sympathies, religious and political, were thus defiantly wounded and outraged.

... One observation more we think it necessary to make, and that is in reference to the statement reiterated in so many journals, to the effect that Cardinal Wiseman and the Catholic priests in general had instigated and stimulated their flocks to the part taken by them in the Hyde Park and Birkenhead riots. A more silly and groundless charge it would be impossible to fabricate. Do not the Catholic priests, even if they desired (which they do not) the people to engage in riots and disorders, know how fatal they would prove to them? Do they not know the laws properly forbid such tumults, that the force is overwhelming which the Irish have to encounter, and to which they must needs succumb? Have not the Catholic priests, in fine, whether in England or in Ireland, uniformly exerted all their influence and authority to prevent such outbreaks? Charges of this kind are therefore as malicious as they are untrue. But they are calculated to increase the hostility felt in England towards the Catholic clergy, and this is probably the intention of their vilifiers.[105]

The meeting began at 7pm and finished at 9.30pm. During this time the Birkenhead police patrolled the streets around the church and dispersed crowds as they gathered. They were performing a civil police role, preventing conflict and taking the odd prisoner when an opportunity presented itself. At this point presumably the magistrates thought they had matters well in hand. The armed Orange contingent marched off to the ferry, having decided their contribution was no longer needed:

> There is no doubt [they] were prepared for a 'row', they took no visible part in the affray. They returned to Liverpool between nine and ten o'clock. They stopped at the residence of Mr Laird, MP, and they gave three cheers for the honourable gentleman, which they followed up with cheers for Garibaldi and the Queen.[106]

The Cheshire police had been guarding the church. About 10 o'clock they joined their Birkenhead colleagues, and it was they who took the decision to charge a crowd who were throwing missiles. Most of the violence followed this incident, much of it and over half the arrests took place in Oak Street. They were performing a rather different role, in military terms they were 'taking the fight to the enemy', under the command of the ex-military leader, Captain Smith.

Oak Street had a reputation for disorder. The census returns of 1861 show it to have been inhabited entirely by Irish labourers and their families. In England as in Ireland Irish Catholics tended to respond as a relatively cohesive community to aggressive policing. The tactic of setting fire to chimneys to create smoke and reduce visibility was employed in 1862, This also ensured there were no witnesses to police action.

The police account of 1862 was of heavy and persistent stoning from inside the houses. Two houses were broken into, and their

---

[105] Catholic Telegraph, 25th October, 1862

[106] Liverpool Courier, 15th October, 1862

inhabitants arrested. One of them, Patrick Fahey, aged sixty, was dragged naked through the streets to the town hall. He had evidently been rioting from his bed.

However, what was important was not what happened on that night, but what people said and believed about what had happened. Information about events was not controlled by the magistrates. Indeed, there is evidence that the magistrates were reasonably pleased by the way things had gone. Their major objectives had been attained and, despite police complaints of their extensive casualty list, there had been no fatalities. They were certainly surprised by the storm of criticism unleashed at them. The forces that had transmuted 'another Irish row' on October 8th into a riot that threatened the basis of British civilisation were now directed at the magistrates themselves. The descriptions of 'Irish savagery' promoted by Dr Baylee, and belatedly adopted by John Laird, were to become dominant in public discussion of what had happened on the night of October 15, 1862.

There could be no better indication in the 19th century that a particular account had become dominant among competing accounts that it should be adopted in a Times leader:

> It is plain that the greatest pusillanimity prevailed among those who held the power, but not the discrimination to enforce the law. It is equally plain that, if order and the rights of Englishmen to free speech are to be preserved, bolder and sterner courses must be taken with wretches like the Birkenhead Irish. In any city on the continent, in any city of the United States, an organised body attacking the authorities of the town would have been fired upon and dispersed by the troops. If the Riot Act had been read, and the soldiers from Manchester had done their duty, this tumult would have been over at once and those unhappy policemen who now lie in danger of death, never have been sacrificed. As it is, the inefficiency of the magistrates has exposed a great town to bloodshed and pillage and given the popish priests of the place the power to triumph in their

> victory over English liberty and law.[107]

The views of The Times were challenged in a letter from 'A Cheshire Magistrate'. This was probably Major General Sir Edward Cust, Chairman of the Birkenhead Magistrates, ex-soldier, author, resident of Leasowe Castle and Master of Ceremonies at Queen Victoria's court. He wrote:

> The object of the precautions… was to protect the proceedings of a debating society which … had been assailed by a lawless mob. This object ... was fully attained. The force on the ground had been such as to render any attempt at molestation perfectly futile. It was no doubt from a conviction of this, that the mob commenced rioting at some distance from the spot in question.
>
> As regards the charge of not ordering the special constables forward to attack the mob … I can only say that … I should have been very reluctant to give any such order, as it became very evident … that many of them were activated less by a desire to keep the public peace than by a strong partisan feeling, such as could hardly have failed to render the conflict a most formidable and fatal one.[108]

Cust was well aware of the dangers of organised Protestant violence. Stockport in 1852 had seen an outbreak resulting in murder and wrecked houses and churches. His analysis was confirmed by the two clerks to the Birkenhead magistrates, who wrote to the Times:

> The magistrates, however, were satisfied that the police force was sufficient to restore order without other aid, and the results prove they were right… The supposition that the mob obtained a triumph is altogether a mistake. The police, as they were

107 The Times, 30th October, 1862

108 Liverpool Mercury, 20th October, 1862

> justified, freely used their truncheons. ... The intended meeting was quietly held, the row was entirely suppressed, and before midnight the town was perfectly quiet.[109]

According to the Birkenhead magistrates, and they were the people on the ground and responsible for public order, there never were any Garibaldi Riots in Birkenhead. Unarmed police, still essentially preventative in character and not a militia, had kept order. The dominant view was of organised and dangerous riots, in contrast the magistrates talked of a disorderly mob engaged in a 'row.' The whole issue had been sensationalized, especially by the police, keen to promote their own heroism.

Attempts were made to humiliate Sir Edward Cust, both personally and politically. The newspapers reported with some glee one occasion when he opened a letter in court which contained a white feather, and another occasion when he opened the parcel containing a lady's petticoat.

The Chester Chronicle, which recognised the peculiar religious politics of Liverpool and Birkenhead, took a more nuanced view. Issues of religion were central to Irish identities in the 19th century, perhaps even transcending class and economic rivalry. The first thing that one Irish person wished to know about another was what religion they were. Irish people in Ireland had become involved in entrenched hostility between religious groups. That hostility had been transferred to parts of England especially through the number of appointments of Irish Evangelicals in the bishopric of Chester.

The alarmist reporting in the Liverpool Mail, The Times, and to a lesser extent the Liverpool Mercury, had its consequences for the town of Birkenhead. On the 25th of October, the Cheshire Observer reported on the condition of Birkenhead:

> During the week the township of Birkenhead has been in a constant state of excitement, and grave fears have been entertained that some serious outbreak would take place, but happily there has been no

[109] The Times, 22nd October, 1862

> disturbance. We cannot but express an opinion that much of the alarm that has prevailed may be traced to the circulation of not only false, but absurd reports as to the intentions of Roman Catholics, and which in too many cases have found too ready a circulation in the columns of certain newspapers on the other side of the Mersey, and would seem to have made it a study to magnify the dangers and feed the excitement. We think the opposite course should have been pursued, for no good can result at any time from the use of irritating language and particularly when men's minds are somewhat excited.[110]

On 24 October 1862, under the headline, 'FURTHER APPREHENDED RIOTS AT BIRKENHEAD AND CLAUGHTON - LECTURE BY THE REV DR BUTLER'[111] , the Liverpool Mercury reported that green placards were being put up around Birkenhead. Their message was:

> Irishmen and Catholics - we earnestly request you to stay at home this evening to go to no meetings; to give your enemies no opportunity and avoid standing at the street corners or elsewhere. Irishmen and Catholics, obey your pastors.
>
> R. Canon Chapman, R W Brundit, Eugene Busquet.
> St Werburgh's October 23, 1862.[112]

There was to be a lecture in the evening of Thursday, October 23rd at Christ Church Claughton, which was then a village just outside of the jurisdiction of the Birkenhead magistrates. The Vicar of Christ Church was Rev Dr Blakeney. Earlier in the month he had invited Liverpool Orangemen to help police the supposed Garibaldi Riot. The lecture was to be on "Rome and Popery." It was to be given by Dr Butler, in the 1830s and early 1840s he was an opponent of M'Neile and Baylee but he was now Baylee's ally.

---

110 Cheshire Observer, 25th October, 1862

111 Liverpool Mercury, 24th October, 1862

112 Ibid

Blakeney applied to the Cheshire magistrates for protection. On the evening of the meeting there were 175 constables of the County police around Christ Church. 300 special constables had been sworn in from the area. There were also regular troops held in reserve with their firearms loaded and fixed bayonets. This was the military option. Birkenhead town police armed with cutlasses were stationed at the boundary of Birkenhead and Claughton. This was much the same deployment as on 15 October. It was an obvious provocation.

On the evening of the meeting, Dr Blakeney introduced Butler. He pointed out, in his normal conciliatory fashion that unless they stood up to the threats to civil liberty that Irish Catholics represented, then any Bible or Missionary meeting was at threat. According to him Protestants were being persecuted:

> The fact was, the principles of the Church of Rome were hostile to civil and religious liberty. (Cheers.) They had heard that men were thrust into dungeons in Spain simply because they were Protestants and would read the Bible; and if ever the principles of Romanism which prevailed in Spain should triumph in this country their liberty would be vanquished and destroyed. (Cheers.) ... An effort had been made by terrorism to put down the present meeting. (Reiterated cheering.)
>
> If they thus relinquished their rights, then the anniversary meeting of a bible or a missionary society would be the signal for the rising of a mob, who might prevent such meeting, and this might lead ultimately even to the closing of the churches by mob law, if it was allowed to continue. he felt they would gain nothing by deferring the struggle; on the contrary they should be weakened for encounter when it arrived, and he therefore determined to the utmost of his power to maintain his rights. (Cheers.)
>
> Dr Butler began his speech which was, apparently, mainly about the principal buildings in Rome, but did manage to condemn the tyranny of the Pope and the oppression and degradation of the people it

> entailed.[113]

At the conclusion of the meeting, Dr Blakeney asked the audience to depart peaceably.

> Immediately a cry was raised by the Orangemen for the muster of their forces outside the church and the men fell into marching order about five abreast. At this time, the cudgels, with which many of them were armed were drawn from their pockets and from beneath their upper clothing...The procession passed down Oxton Road, through Grange Lane, and Hamilton Street to the ferry ... immediately they began their march the firing of pistols, with which many were armed, was commenced A short distance from this mob, a body of twenty policemen marched armed with cutlasses, but they did not interfere. ... On passing the Catholic chapel, groans were given for the Pope, and several firearms were exploded... the crowd slackened for a moment, opposite the residence of John Laird, Esq. M.P, for whom three hearty cheers were given, with a similar compliment for Garibaldi, and three groans for the Pope.[114]

It is difficult to imagine a more provocative sequence of events. Dr Blakeney was not, as he claimed, saving freedom of speech and worship with the assistance of a mercenary apostate Catholic priest. Rather, the whole affair had been an act of Orange triumphalism connived at by the Birkenhead police force, the Cheshire force, the military authorities, and presumably, by John Laird and at least some of the Birkenhead Commissioners. In this respect, it had much in common with the so-called Garibaldi Riots earlier in the month. It could be said that this point marked the triumph of bigotry. Despite extreme provocation, the "Croppies" had lain down. If Orangemen had

---

113 Cheshire Observer, 25th October, 1862

114 Ibid

wondered what they could get away with in Birkenhead, they now knew. It could include threatening behaviour, carrying and letting off of firearms, and even incitement to riot. The town had been made safe from Catholics.

"Porcupine", a Liverpool satirical magazine presented an alternative view of the triumph of 'free speech':

> THE PAPAL POT AND THE ORANGE KETTLE
>
> Porcupine has a strong aversion to Roman Catholic fanaticism for many reasons; but if he were asked to give the reason why, at the present day, he most detested, he rather thinks he would answer - "Because of the impulse it gives to Orange bigotry".
>
> In itself, papalist fervour can really do little serious harm nowadays. The Inquisition cannot be established in Birkenhead... but papalist bigotry, which is in itself bad, can let loose Orange bigotry, which is in itself somewhat worse. Orangemen are just as blatant, silly, unreasoning, arrogant, and tyrannical as papalists, and they have (amongst us at least) very much more influence. Look at the state of things in Birkenhead! The reign of the shillelagh has scarcely closed when the anarchy of the Orange bludgeon set in. We entirely object to meeting bigotry with bigotry, and do not at all approve of the sort of public protection which is obtained by setting an Orange mob to rabble a popish mob. Plague on both their houses say we.
>
> ... That was an amazingly silly demonstration which took place in Birkenhead the other night, when a gentleman named Butler favoured the community with his opinions upon the Pope, and a grand demonstration of moral force, in the shape of Orangemen armed with bludgeons, was made in order to secure to Birkenhead the inestimable boon of Mr Butler's eloquence. Understand that we are for the fullest right of public meeting and speech. If it be necessary, if even anybody thinks it necessary, to

hold a meeting and denounce the Pope in Birkenhead, that meeting has a right to full protection, and any ruffian who interrupted by force of cudgel ought to have a spell on the treadmill. But was there much of good feeling in getting up an anti-papal lecture and demonstration in Birkenhead just at the present moment? A meeting held at a very appropriate time to express sympathy with Garibaldi is quite a different thing from an aggressive harangue by a professed no-popery lecturer, just as a defence of the right of free speech is entirely unlike a procession of cudgel armed Orangemen firing pistols and giving groans for the Pope as they pass the Roman Catholic Chapel. What is sauce for the Catholic goose is sauce for the Protestant gander; and if Teddy Maloney, from Cork, must not make a physical display in the streets of Birkenhead, neither must Sandy Macraw, the Orangeman from the black north. Besides, we enlightened Protestants are supposed to know how to sustain order properly - are we not, Macraw? And we are true Christians, not like those poor deluded papists, and we know that the mission of Christ was peace - don't we Dr Blakeney? And we are for equal freedom and equal privileges to all, not like the ultramontanes - aren't we Dr Butler? We really think Dr Butler himself might have postponed his lecture to another season without any infraction whatever of his duty as a citizen and a Christian; and we do not think Dr Blakeney acted either generously or kindly in organising such a demonstration at such a time.

We certainly ought not to endeavour to make our Irish brother offend, especially when we have come prepared with a preponderance of bludgeons. To be sure, Dr Blakeney requested all his friends to go home quietly, but the Roman Catholic priests, too, always make the same kind of requests. Only excited crowds do not always obey such injunctions; and ministers of religion who ought to understand such things pretty well, should endeavour to avoid demonstrations in which the preservation of the public peace depends on the chance of an unroused rabble obeying a polite pastoral request to begone ... and not kick up a row.

Besides, we distrust Orangemen as preservers of the peace. Since when have they taken on themselves this unwonted task? Their part has not usually been anything of that meek nature. Belfast and Derry, Coleraine and Dollysbrae, still tell some tales of Orange prowess which do not display much of a pacificatory tendency. Even in Liverpool itself have we not had processions of rowdy-looking individuals armed with guns, patrolling the streets; and, when banished from the streets, marshalling on the Wavertree Road, flaunting their banners and flourishing their weapons? Was all this done to preserve the public peace - which then no one but themselves disturbed? No, no, the repute which the Orangemen have most vociferously claimed and pertinaciously vindicated, is not that of peacemakers. When we see a gang of these persons marching five abreast, and armed with bludgeons, we cannot for the life of us look upon them as the beneficent and meek guardians of public order. Nor do we believe in the admiration of Garibaldi these people have taken to professing. Garibaldi is not at all the hero who suits a rabble of bludgeon-men. He is an intense lover of peace, - a votary of goodwill to all, love and heroic devotion make up the chief part of his noble character. It sickens us to hear his illustrious name profaned by a gang of characters whose chief ambition would be - if they only had the chance - to pitch-cap or hang up everyone who dared to differ from them. Garibaldi represents full liberty of opinion, and when has the Orange faction represented ought but the most arrogant and malignant dominancy? ... It is quite time to repudiate

> such companionship. If order is to be kept in Birkenhead at all, let it be by the agency of the proper authorities, and not be by the braggadocio of a coarse and virulent mob. Let us have the papists kept down by persons who will not patrol the neighbourhood groaning for the Pope. We cannot have Birkenhead converted into another Dollysbrae or Sandy Row. We altogether demur to calling in the garroters to defend us from the burglars. Put down rioters of all classes. A fellow is not to be allowed to endanger the permanent peace of the whole community simply because he is provoking a row for the sake of enforcing order. If there are not police enough in Birkenhead to secure the town against riot, let more force be obtained somewhere. Better by far, the Riot Act and a bayonet charge or two, than the Orange mob to start into active existence under the pretence of maintaining public order. The whole thing is unspeakably disgraceful to a civilised community, and, on the whole, we think the Blakeney and Butler riot rather more disreputable than the other. A "row" can occur in the best ordered place; but the character of the locality is shown by the means to preserve order and put the disturbance down. If the people of Birkenhead can devise no better means of securing freedom of speech, than turning out a howling Orange mob to scare into silence a less powerful Papist mob, the place does not deserve to be classed among civilized and Christian communities.[115]

The way in which this incident was handled, does however echo other incidents in Birkenhead's then recent past, in which John Laird was involved, in particular the use of special constables, the importation of Orange 'muscle' from Liverpool, and the cooperation of that 'muscle' with the local police.

The Cheshire Observer ran an editorial headlined:

---

115 The Porcupine, 1st November, 1862

THE BIRKENHEAD RIOTS

We hope, and firmly believe, that we have seen the end of the Birkenhead riots, and sincerely trust that any ill-feeling which they may have engendered will pass away, and that people may resume those kindly feelings one towards another which should ever characterise citizens. If the Roman Catholic population, or any part of them, were really the originators of the strife, then the closing scene by no means reflects credit upon their Protestant brethren. It was almost as sorry a sight to witness the crowds of men who perambulated the streets of Birkenhead on Thursday night armed with deadly weapons procured for the purpose of dashing out the brains of Roman Catholics, as it was to witness the riots and confusion that prevailed eight days before and laid to their charge. Surely such proceedings as have been witnessed in Birkenhead during the last fortnight cannot have the sanction of the respectable members or professors of either creed. We can imagine nothing more dangerous than the proceedings taken by the Orangemen of Liverpool on Thursday, in visiting Birkenhead, armed as they were, and the inhabitants have indeed cause to be thankful that no collision took place, for had a conflict once commenced there is no telling to what extent it would have gone, or what number of valuable lives would have been sacrificed.[116]

Rev Brundit defended his conduct in a letter to The Times:

THE BIRKENHEAD RIOTS

TO THE EDITOR OF THE TIMES

SIR- Permit me, through the medium of your widely circulated columns, to say a few words in

[116] Cheshire Observer, 25th October, 1862

answer to many accusers. Three grave crimes are especially laid to my charge: That I made a speech on Wednesday, the 8th instant, in which I told a riotous mob that they had done quite right in smashing the windows of a school and church. That on Wednesday, the 15th instant, I incited a mob to attack and ill-use the police. That, in a letter which I wrote to the Liverpool Daily Post and Mercury on the 14th instant, I declared that I would not if I could, "Step forward to prevent the maiming or murdering of fellow creatures."

Allow me, Sir, to answer: That in the speech I made on Wednesday, the 8th instant, I told the mob that they had no right to interrupt the meeting of the Parliamentary Debating Society, and, so even though they had been irritated by the nature of the placards calling the meeting, and that that society has as much right to meet and discuss any question as we had to meet for our own purposes. Many Protestants who heard me can bear witness that this was the burthen of my harangue. That on Wednesday, the 15th instant, I was never out of the house or church (neither of which is within half a mile of the scene of the riot) after 4 p.m. This can be proved by several witnesses.

This charge I flatly deny. I am not and will not be responsible for every or any gloss which ignorance or prejudice may put up on my words. I exercised my privilege as an Englishman to choose whether I would act as policeman or not. It is not to my taste to go among excited mobs, and, as it was well known that hundreds of Orangemen had arranged to come over from Liverpool, I thought that the presence of a priest would only be an extra incitement to keep them to cause a row, and so I threw the task of keeping the peace upon its legitimate guardians. In addition, considering the service I had rendered Dr Baylee and his ingratitude, and that my actions, words, and motives had all been misrepresented by him and by others, I thought it the more prudent part not again to interfere or to expose myself to their malice.

While addressing you, and through you, I hope thousands of my fellow countrymen who like to hear both sides of a question, permit me further to state, that I had no reason to apprehend any disturbance upon the part of the Catholics on Wednesday, the 15th instant, but, on the contrary, I had every reason to hope that they would respond to my wishes and stay in their houses. Some 200 or 300 unfortunately, went to the neighbourhood of the meeting; but I am informed, both by Protestants and Catholics, that had not the police commenced the row, and most savagely attacked and knocked down quiet lookers-on, no such disgraceful scenes as afterwards occurred would have been witnessed.

Throughout these disturbances I have, by personal visitation among the people and by entreaty from the pulpit, done all in my power to keep them quiet, and no one has throughout regretted more than I the lawless scenes which have been enacted.

Everyone knows the excitable temperament of the Irish, and no one better than Drs Baylee and Blakeney, themselves Irishmen. I put it, then, to the calm judgements of my countrymen, whether (granted, if it so please, the misconduct of the mob on the previous Wednesday) any Christian of any denomination can do otherwise than regret that that second meeting was held in the excited state of the township, and in opposition to the wishes of the local authorities, and that Dr Butler, an apostate priest, should be brought into the town to keep up the excitement, and still further to irritate the Catholics.- I am, sir, yours etc.

Robert Wright Brundrit, M.A., Cambridge. St. Werburgh's, Birkenhead, Oct. 24.

> P.S. Dr Butler gave his lecture on Rome and Popery last night. the Liverpool daily papers of today state that a large party of Orangemen from Liverpool (about 500), "did their best to provoke a collision by firing pistols constantly and calling out 'Where are the Birkenhead rioters now?' and calling for cheers for the Birkenhead police and Garibaldi, and loud groans for the Pope. Every man in this Orange mob carried a weapon of some sort or another". "On passing the Catholic Chapel groans were given for the Pope and several firearms were exploded. ``In addition to this band of Orangemen, hundreds of young men, evidently of the more respectable classes, thronged the footways with bludgeons in hand, ready to second any efforts which might be made to thrash the Irishmen. We are glad to say that a wise discretion was exercised by those parties keeping out of sight so as to render a collision impossible." Who were the aggressors last night? and why were none of these riotous miscreants apprehended? Was it because they cheered the police? One extract more. When these "supporters of law and good order", as Dr Blakeney had just called them, got to the ferry boat, "a stalwart policeman went up to the body of the men, and accosting them in a friendly spirit, congratulated them upon the way they had conducted themselves". What next?[117]

What the incident demonstrated was that the Birkenhead police, or some of them at least, were aware of how to defuse a potentially violent situation. The Orangemen were approached in a friendly manner. The policeman made it clear that no one desired conflict. He did not try to disarm anyone, even though some were carrying illegal weapons. He showed he understood Orange grievances, he even shared them. It was clear that the police and other authorities in Birkenhead made no effort to understand Catholic grievances even

[117] The Times, October 24th, 1862

though Catholic intentions were not murderous, unlike those of the Orangemen.

In the period before trial, an alternative view of the disturbances was presented to the public in The Tablet, a Catholic newspaper. Canon Chapman organised a Defence Fund and appealed for money to pay for representation of the accused. He addressed those Catholics who considered the arrested 'a bad lot', who deserved what was coming to them:

> Falsehood can be printed as well as written...there are about twenty poor men and women in Chester Castle on a charge of rioting. Most of these men and all these women were dragged from their houses and some even from their beds without a rag on their backs by policemen, goaded to savagery by the taunts of prejudiced and ill-informed reporters and editors of unprincipled newspapers – and on the oaths of these brutal policemen, committed by magistrates who had not the manly courage to allow a word to be said in defence of these victims of police vengeance.[118]

The one-time supporter of the Conservative Party and the established order began to display a deep cynicism about the corruption, which maintained that order. How he must have regretted the triumphalism of his march to the polls which had brought such Conservative acrimony down on him and his parishioners. In November 1862, under the headline "Birkenhead Police Riots", Canon Chapman continued his appeal for funds to pay for the defence of:

> ... Eighteen unfortunate Irishmen, accused and severely punished for a row, brought up by Irish parsons and policemen. The witnesses for the prosecution will be not less than fifty, composed of policemen, hard swearers on such occasions – ladies of doubtful character, prompted by offer of rewards

[118] The Tablet, 6th December, 1862

> on conviction, and medical men who will, no doubt, bear witness to the blood and wounds, and other horrible things, and how bruises and gashes were inflicted by stalwart Irishmen – making very lucid distinction between the blow of a policeman's baton and that of a brickbat.[119]

From the outset the Birkenhead magistrates were determined to deny those accused of rioting a fair hearing. Witnesses for the defence were not heard and prosecution witnesses were not questioned, defence lawyers were sometimes denied the right to represent their clients before the magistrates.

The main prosecution witness in the case that is outlined below was the landlord of the British Queen Hotel. His evidence was mainly directed at James Fynan who, for a man of sixty-five, appeared by the landlord's account to be surprisingly energetic.

> THE BIRKENHEAD RIOTERS.
>
> Yesterday, at the Birkenhead police court, before Messrs. Young husband and H. Segar, junior, James Fynan (an elderly man), Bridget Burns, Mary Burns, and Bridget McDonald, were brought up on remand; charged with having been concerned in the riots in the township on the night of Wednesday, the 15th inst. The women, who were tolerably well- dressed, had each a child in her arms. Mr Bell and Mr Pemberton appeared to prosecute, and Mr B. Moore defended the prisoners.
>
> Mr William Smith, proprietor of the British Queen Hotel, Watson-street, said that on Wednesday, the 15th Inst., between seven and eight o'clock in the evening, there was a great moving crowd in front of his premises; the first stone was thrown at his house at a quarter to eight o'clock. When he saw the crowd becoming very boisterous, he secured his doors and pulled down his blinds. The mob were shouting,

---

119 Birkenhead News, 1st Nov, 1862

yelling, and running about. Directly after the first stone was thrown, he put out the gas in all the rooms. Immediately afterwards the stones and brickbats entered his premises like a shower of rain. The mob continued shouting and throwing stones until nearly every window in the house was broken. After the windows were broken, he sheltered himself behind a wall in a passage, and kept looking into the spirit vaults. He saw the prisoner Fynan amongst the mob in Watson-Street just before the first charge of the police down Price Street. At the time Fynan was in his shirt sleeves, had on a billycock hat, and had a stick in his hand. He was shouting, "Here's a Garibaldi, here's a Garibaldi," and was throwing his arms up. There was a great crowd of men and women with him, all of them shouting and yelling. One of the brickbats that was thrown against the windows struck him (witnessed), on the forehead, but it did him no harm. He knew Fynan for twelve or fourteen years. He saw several women at the corner of Appleton Court breaking bricks, and bricks were also being broken underneath his windows for nearly two hours. He heard a cry "The police, the police',' and the mob then seemed to congregate. A stone having been then thrown at his windows, he heard someone shout, "Throw no more stones there, for the glass is all broken, but save them for the police." Between nine and ten o'clock, he heard a horse and cart come twice into Watson Street with each time a load of macadam, which he distinctly heard upset in the street. Fynan was in the habit of calling at the witness's house for three years, to collect subscriptions for the Roman Catholic schools and other charitable purposes. The witness freely contributed towards these charities, and frequently gave him money for sick purposes. He had no doubt that Fynan was the man who was in Watson Street in his shirt sleeves leading the mob.

Daniel Prescott, barman and ostler in the employ of the previous witness, said he went to the window in Price-street, and in looking through saw the mob throwing stones. The prisoner Fynan was leading them In his shirt sleeves. He had on a billycock hat, and had a stick in one hand, and a stone or brick in the other. He shouted, "This way, lads". The mob then went a little way up Price Street and returned. Saw Fynan throw a stone at the police. Had no doubt that Fynan was the man.

A woman, named Mary Ebery, deposed that she saw the three female prisoners throw stones at the British Queen Hotel on the night in question. Detective-officer Elliott Hodgson deposed to having apprehended the prisoner on Tuesday night last, under a warrant. He took him to the Police office, where he was observed putting two books into his breast pocket. In going to the bridewell he threw over the wall in Hamilton street the two books, which witness produced. The books authorised the holder to receive subscriptions towards "a fair trial fund", and was signed “J. F O'Neile, hon. sec." In the house of the prisoner Maguire witness found a small tin biscuit box, which was supposed to have been stolen from the shop of Mr Coulter on the night of the riots.

This being the whole of the evidence for the prosecution, Mr Moore proposed to call a number of witnesses for the defence, and urged that it was hardly justice for the bench to refuse hearing his evidence, Mr Younghusband said there was conflicting evidence, and it would be for a jury to decide the case. Mr Moore replied that he had several respectable witnesses whom he would tender to prove that Mr Smith and his barman were mistaken as to Fynan being with the mob. He had also evidence to prove an alibi with respect to the other prisoners. Mr Younghusband remarked that if Mr Moore produced 500 persons to prove an alibi the magistrates could not reject the evidence they had already heard.

Mr Moore: 'I have three witnesses against one'. Mr Younghusband: 'That may be. It is a question as to the preponderance of evidence, and the jury are the proper parties to decide'.

Mr Moore urged that he was entitled to have the evidence of the witnesses for the defence placed on the depositions, in order that it might go before the judge. He then quoted from "Saunders' Petty Sessions", to show that it was the duty of the magistrates to hear witnesses for the defence. Mr Townsend (the clerk to the magistrates) said he had a strong opinion as to the law of the case, and he wished Mr Moore would apply for a mandamus on the subject. He had frequently considered the matter with great care. He had looked over the whole of Jarvis's Act with reference to this point, and from one end to the other it did not say one word about the prisoner. In the clause relating to the binding over of witnesses it stated that when all the witnesses for the prosecution were examined, then something shall be done; but there was not one word about witnesses for the defence. His opinion was that such a thing was never contemplated. Another clause directed the principle which should guide magistrates in sending prisoners for trials, and that principle was to ascertain whether there was a prima facie case to send the accused to trial, Mr Pemberton contended that it was discretionary with the magistrates whether they should hear witnesses for the defence.

After some further discussion, Mr Moore tendered his witnesses for examination, but the bench refused to receive their evidence. The prisoners then made statements to the effect that they had no connection with the mob; that they threw neither stones nor brickbats; and that they were in their own houses at the time spoken to by the witnesses. With regard to

> them collecting books, Fynan said he "had them in his possession to give to other people who were innocent as well as himself."
>
> The four prisoners were then committed for trial at the Chester Assizes. Bail was refused, the magistrates stating that they would be guided in this case by the decision of the bench on Saturday last. Mr Moore gave notice that he would renew his application to admit the whole of the prisoners to bail on Thursday next, at the petty sessions.[120]

If he was entrusted with collecting for Catholic charities, Fynan must have been a community leader for Catholics in Birkenhead and closely associated with Catholic clergy. The reason he threw the collecting books away, was a suspicion the contributors to the defence fund were vulnerable to arrest. Now elderly community leaders who are closely associated, perhaps friends of Canon Chapman, would be unlikely to be leaders of mobs. But they would be highly likely to be targets for police and a magistracy, looking for revenge on a Catholic community, which had dragged the reputation of both bodies through the mud.

The behaviour of the magistrates was, at times, of dubious legality. In the next case to be examined, Mr Derbyshire, the same Mr Derbyshire who had declared himself an ultra-Protestant at John Laird's victory banquet, had used a summary court as a sessions court. Summary courts were used to try and sentence people for minor offences such as drunk and disorderly. Major offences, such as riot, were heard initially in sessions courts, as a preliminary to being tried before a judge and jury at a quarter sessions.

The evidence of the one witness whose word was enough to have three people locked up, was fairly obviously tainted. She had been rewarded a huge sum of money, £50, to give evidence. Against one of the defendants, she had an obvious grievance. The defendant had gone off with her lodger.

> THE LATE RIOTS AT BIRKENHEAD. POLICE COURT, MONDAY, Nov. 24,

[120] Liverpool Mercury, 29th Oct, 1862

Mr Bretherton stated that some parties had been apprehended last night, for having been participators in the late riots at Birkenhead. He said one had been dragged from his bed at eleven o'clock at night, and others at unreasonable hours, although these people had never been absent from the town since the occurrence, and although they would have been quite ready to answer any warrant that might have been taken out against them. The way in which the police were proceeding was a certain way to lead to a disturbance. The presiding magistrate, R. Bryan, Esq., said this was the first he had heard of the arrests. Mr Bretherton: Very likely, but the names of the parties and the offence charged against them should appear on the sheet then before them. The names of the parties were Moses Doyle, and Patrick Doyle. Detective Hodgson: There is a third, Ann Canty. Mr Bretherton: They ought to be brought up here as this is the sessions court. Mr Bryan: We have just learned that the matter has been before Mr Derbyshire this morning and he has entered the cases as remanded until tomorrow. The Inspector of Police applied for a remand. Detective Hodgson said the prisoners were not defended. Mr Bretherton wished to know if there were to be two courts on Mondays and Thursdays. Mr Townsend, magistrates' clerk, said that on those days' summary cases, the drunk and disorderly were taken at the other court for the purpose of clearing the lock up. Mr Bretherton: But other cases appear to have been taken, and they as advocates, and the public must be informed as to the practice. Mr Townsend: on Mondays and Thursdays at the other court the drunk and disorderly cases are taken. Mr Bretherton: But this case does not come under that category. Mr Townsend: If you will allow me to finish, Mr Bretherton, I will explain that other cases are preliminarily inquired into and remands ordered, as was the case that day. Mr Bretherton said it was unfair to prisoners to be brought up in the way they had been in the absence of witnesses. He applied that the hearing of the case in question might be taken on Thursday. Mr Bryan (presiding magistrate): We grant the application. The prisoners will be brought up proforma tomorrow and will be remanded until Thursday.

Wednesday, Nov 24. Moses and Patrick Doyle, and Ann Casey were brought up on remand with being concerned in the late riots on the 15th of October. Mr Bell appeared for the prosecution, and Mr Bretherton for the defence. The first witness for the prosecution was Elizabeth Richardson, lately residing at 51 St. Anne's Street, deposed to the general facts of the riot and that she saw the two male prisoners throw stones or bricks into Mr Coulter's shop, and bring some boxes, like starch boxes, up Watson Street. She also saw the female prisoner get up some bricks from a wall in an entry and throw them through Mr Martin's shop window. In cross-examination by Mr Bretherton, the witness stated that she had first given information to the police three weeks ago on Friday. Went to buy a key at Mr Hills and saw P.C. Cartwright and another officer and told them. She was going to leave her house as her lodgers had left her, and she was afraid to stop. He asked her why, and she told him she had been threatened to be stoned to death and her house burnt under her. Had not been threatened herself. Was in the house up to last Tuesday week. That is from the 15th of October to the 18th of November. Mr Cartwright asked her what she had seen at the riot, and she answered a good deal. Had seen the two young men as usual. Could not say she had seen them every day. Mr Cartwright told her she ought to report on the parties. He did not tell her there was a reward offered. Can read and write. Heard other parties say there was a reward. Received a message to go to the

Town Hall and went. Detective Hodgson asked her what she had seen, and the name of the parties, but she would not tell them, as she was afraid, but would let him know again. About a week or nine days ago went to the office and gave him the names. On Saturday evening last, Margaret Mclntyre and witness went to Oxton to visit a friend, and Mclntyre took her to a beer house called the Raven Hotel. Said there was a woman in St. Anne Street, who had been scandalising her by saying she had gone from there with another man. Did not tell her there were several parties in the street she could do harm to but did tell her that she (witness) had a good mind to do so. Mclntyre said that if she had been threatened as much as witness, she would have had them up. Asked her will you stand by me and tell what you heard in my house. Did not then say if you will be witness for her, she would give Mclntyre part of the money. She was to get £50 but did say if you tell the truth she (witness) would not forget her, but would make her a present, perhaps a sovereign, before the week was out. Mclntyre laughed and said, "Oh, that would make me quite a lady". William Coulter said his shop was broken into and some starch, loaves, etc., had gone. In cross-examination by Mr Bretherton, he stated that he had known the two Doyles and he believed that they had worked for him. Did not know anything against them. Mr Bretherton then addressed the bench on behalf of the prisoners and said he did not know how they could convict the prisoners on the evidence of that one woman unsupported by any other person. She had been bartering for their conviction with another woman. Mr Coulter, one of the witnesses for the prosecution, could not say a word against either of the prisoners. They had been taken out of their beds at the dead of the night, after 11 o'clock. He would produce witnesses to show that the Doyles had been

> in their own house all the night in question and that the prisoner Casey had been with Mrs Richardson's lodger. Mr Bretherton called several witnesses, who fully proved that the Doyles were in their own house and had not gone out beyond the door on the night in question. The bench said that after having carefully considered the case they had decided that they were not justified in committing the prisoners on the evidence of that one witness, and they were therefore discharged. On the prisoners being set at liberty the crowd in the court set up a loud cheer. Cheshire Observer.[121]

It seems obvious that some of the magistrates hearing cases in Birkenhead, would accept the most slender and dubious evidence. Evidence that would not stand up to the scrutiny of a lawyer was initially accepted, after all it was only the lives of Irish Catholics that they were wrecking.

[121] The Tablet, Saturday, December 6th, 1862

CHAPTER EIGHT

The Trials

The canon's misgivings about his people being prepared for "... sacrifice on the altar of bigotry" were to prove well founded. The trials were held in Chester in December 1862 at the winter assizes.

> TUESDAY
>
> The whole of the persons charged with riot in Birkenhead were brought up for trial this morning, his Lordship taking his seat up on the bench at a quarter past nine o'clock. The names of the accused were Patrick Fahey the elder (aged 66), Patrick Fahey the younger (aged 24), James Tracey (aged 23), Thomas Shovelin (aged 19), Elizabeth Curtis (aged 36), Thomas Buckley (aged 40), Michael Fahey (aged 18), John Gorman (aged 26), Thomas Larkin (aged 46), Michael Hogan (aged 18), Michael Martin (aged 47), Catherine Larkin (aged 44), Michael Hoare (aged 35), James Fynan (aged 65), Bridget Burns (aged 32), Henry Lennon (aged 37), Margaret Maguire (aged 30), and Bridget McDonald (aged 22) - All of whom were charged with "unlawfully and riotously assembling, with divers other persons, to the number of twelve and more, to disturb the public peace, and, to the terror and alarm of Her Majesty's subjects at

> Birkenhead, on 15th October last.[122]"

Mr Grove QC opened the case. He said the prisoners were indicted for riot, also for riot and assault, and for unlawful wounding.

Charges of assault were later withdrawn against seventeen of the eighteen in the dock. The evidence for a named prisoner having assaulted a named policeman, was not sufficient to sustain the charges. Henry Lennon had been convicted of assault the day before. He was now in the dock to receive a sentence.

> The Riot Act was not read in fact until a riot existed, and the effect of reading the Riot Act was this - that subsequently to it being read, if the persons did not disperse within an hour, that which otherwise would be a misdemeanour would become a felony. None of the prisoners were charged with felony.[123]

The penalties for misdemeanour were less than those for felony. In this case the maximum was two years. The penalty for a felony could be much greater, up to and including capital punishment.

> Though undoubtedly serious wounds were inflicted ... he was not aware that they could trace home to the prisoners now arraigned (with the exception of Lennon and Hogan, who had been tried), any actual participation in the wounding of any of the police constables. ... Fynan was stated to have been very conspicuous in the riot, flourishing a stick in one hand and a brick in the other. He was seen to break the window of a public house called the British Queen, and he was apparently a very active leader of the rioters, "This way lads, here is a Garibaldi".
>
> Fortunately it was unnecessary to call out the military, and the riot ended without any bloodshed causing death; but undoubtedly a very serious

---

[122] Cheshire Observer, December 20th, 1862

[123] Ibid

> offence was committed, and if such offences could be committed for no other reason that he could find, but because some gentlemen - whether wisely or unwisely, it did not in the least concern them to know - now determined to discuss in a private room, and debate between themselves, some question relating to Garibaldi and the state of Italy, this would cease to be a free country.[124]

Note that to the prosecution, the reasons for Catholics being out on the streets of Birkenhead were inexplicable. That several hundred, armed Orangemen had marched into a Catholic neighbourhood, amongst other provocations, he seems to have deemed irrelevant.

> Something had been said about the colour of the placards issued by the Debating Society; but even if the placards had been purposefully coloured for the purpose alleged, it would be no justification for the riot. ... Bills of that kind were printed of any colour on the mere caprice of the printer and that these were placards of a certain colour was a pure accident.[125]

The prosecutor had certainly not checked this issue with the printer and his statement was tantamount to misleading the jury. Baylee had a long history of posting orange placards.

> In one of the houses where the persons were very volent, and they had no time for consideration, and where if they had waited very long, they would have been killed, they took away one of the prisoners naked. ... But they had been knocked about, they had seen their comrades abused. ... One would think ... that policemen were people to be battered, killed, that they were not human, and were never to lose their tempers under the most serious provocation but

---

[124] Ibid

[125] Ibid

> always to conduct themselves like perfect lambs.[126]

This was how the case for abusing the elderly was justified at Chester Assizes. Witnesses were then called to give evidence for the prosecution.

> William Burgess, one of the county police - on 15th October he was at Birkenhead, and was sent by Captain Smith to the neighbourhood of Price Street; saw 500 or 600 people together headed by a priest, many of them being armed with sticks; they came to about 80 or 100 yards of the institute, were they halted by the direction of the priest who said, "Stay, boys, stop, easy; be quiet boys, we want peace and we'll have peace, but we will have no Garibaldian meeting here tonight." there was a "hurrah" and a tremendous cheer was given for the Pope.[127]

The next witness to give evidence was Inspector Keenan of the Birkenhead police. He was asked by the judge to describe the rioters.

> The mob appeared more like a lot of savages than anything else. Father Goulding addressed the crowd opposite the institute. The substance of the speech ... was as follows: He began by telling them what they had done for the honour and glory of England, the many battles which their forefathers had fought; how they bled and died in their country's cause, and the honour they had contributed to the English nation. He enumerated some of the fields on which Irish fame had been exhibited, mentioning Waterloo, the Crimea, Badajoz, and several other places.

[126] Ibid

[127] Ibid

Navvies as Heroes[128]

> He then told them to give three cheers for the Pope, which they gave; also three cheers for the Queen, which were given; and thirdly, cheers for the British dominions, coupling therewith England, and Ireland, and Scotland. He then raised his hands to them and requested them to go home. They immediately became most outrageous, so much so that all remonstrance on his part was drowned in the yelling and screaming. We then charged them over a cabbage field and scattered them in all directions.[129]

Some discrepancy there, as the defence pointed out in their closing remarks:

> Inspector Rowbottam deposed to being assaulted with stones etc from Fahey's house. He knocked at the door, because it was fast; and he then broke open

[128] Navvies waiting to embark for the Crimean War, there to build a railway, prefabricated at the Canada Works. Illustrated London News, December 20th, 1854

[129] Cheshire Observer, December 20th, 1862

the window and jumped; people rushed through the house. He went upstairs, and found Patrick Fahey Junior, and Michael Fahey under a bed. They had with them an old musket, which appeared to have been recently fired. Some powder and shot were found on one of the Faheys. Cross-examined: In jumping through the window he jumped into a bed with somebody in it; could not say if the gun had been fired on the previous day.

John Slater Martin, a police constable, said he took Patrick Fahey into custody. He had no clothes when he took him. - The Judge: do you mean to say you took him stark naked? Witness: Yes; Fahey had not a thing on when I took him. Cross-examined by Mr Welsby: he had not at that time been sworn in as a constable, and he was in plain clothes.

Ergo Constable John Slater Martin, who at the time was not a constable at all, had no business policing a riot or arresting anybody. Presumably he had gone along for the ride and for the pleasure of beating and shaming Irish people.

In the closing speeches for the defence, the jury heard first from Mr Welsby. He acknowledged that there had been rioting, but in Watson Street, hundreds of yards from Holy Trinity Church. He expressed astonishment that the forces assembled could not have dealt with that. He focused on the issues between the two police inspectors and concluded that the evidence provided by Burgess was simply a lie. He, from his experience of armed and dangerous civil disorder professed himself amazed at the lack of physical evidence of the arms said to have been at the disposal of the rioters.

Mr Welsby rose to address the jury on behalf of his clients. He would embrace this, the earliest opportunity of stating, that the case had been most fairly and openly conducted by the learned counsel for the crown, and with the exception of evidence as to the individual participation of some of the prisoners in the disturbances, the whole case was before them. He did not appear to defend the breach of the law, neither did he appear to say that any man was so ignorant as not to be aware that a body of populace parading the streets, armed, committed a manifest breach of the peace; but he was there to submit for their serious attention, several considerations tending to mitigate very materially the present offence. Learned counsel would be ashamed of his position at the bar of England if he attempted to deny the fact of a riot and serious disturbance. He would not weary them with discussing any of the topics that this sham parliament pretended to argue, neither would he fatigue them with any remarks upon Garibaldi or Italy. Owing to the enormous works in course of construction of Birkenhead, the population was a mixed character, there being a great number of Irishmen employed in the undertaking alluded to; a race patient, industrious, quiet, and contributing largely to the general welfare of the nation, but a race deeply attached to the religion they professed, and deeply attached to the ministers of that religion, and a race that deeply resented any affront, or what they imagine was an affront, offered either to their religion or its clergy. Without entering into the matter of the Orange placards, which circumstances educated people would treat with the contempt such a proceeding deserved, he would simply inform them that these poor ignorant prisoners and their companions would at once believe that an insult to their religion was intended, and that the feelings of the inhabitants were rashly and foolishly provoked by the debating society, which, in no small degree, was reprehensible for its conduct and in no small degree provoked the disturbances that followed. The learned counsel was moved to the greatest astonishment that a riot should have lasted on this occasion for an hour, as, looking at the formidable force of special constables and borough police, county constabulary backed by the presence of the magistrates and a large military force in reserve, he should have considered a disturbance utterly impossible, and he would only ask where were all these people when this wretched mob was in possession of Watson Street? What were they doing? The evidence of Burgess was perfectly astonishing, and had the statements he made been true and confirmed, it would have inflicted on the Rev Mr Goulding's character a stain never to be erased, but most fortunately, the evidence of Burgess was absolutely negated by the testimony of Keenan, and he had no hesitation in saying that Burgess's relation of hearing Mr Goulding address the mob, in the terms stated in his evidence, was entirely a fabrication. It was quite clear which was the testimony of truth. The learned counsel dwelt on the non-production of weapons. On occasions when similar charges, he was sorry to say had been heard in this hall, he had seen the table piled with murderous Instruments of all kinds. Now the only weapon produced was an old, dirty, rusty musket, found in Fahey's house, and which the witness could not say had been discharged that day or the day before. Mr Welsby then commented on the evidence as bearing upon the particular cases of Buckley, Gorman, Fynan, and the Faheys. With respect to old Pat Fahey, the learned counsel said it was an unheard-of and most abominable transaction that he, who had never been seen in connection with the riots in the street that night, should have been dragged naked, a half or three quarters of a mile to the police station. The police constables who went into his house "collared" him, as they said, and the poor aged prisoner was taken in a state "in puris naturalibus" to the bridewell, and, and having been in jail two

> months, he fully anticipated that the jury would let him go home.[130]

James Pope Hennessy, himself an Irish Catholic, and later to be the first Irish Catholic Conservative M.P., gave the jury the benefit of his deeper understanding of Irish enmities and inter-Irish conflict. He understood that Protestant Irish clergymen feared for the future of their Church and their community. The Church of Ireland had for centuries exploited its dominant position, backed by the power of the British army and British directed quasi-military police. By the 1860s that dominance was in question. In 1869, the Church of Ireland was disestablished, that is, it ceased to be the state church in Ireland. People no longer had to pay tithes to it. The British state found itself trying to conciliate Irish Catholic opinion to avoid Irish Catholic rebellion. Irish Protestant clergymen in Birkenhead wanted to encourage repression of Catholics there, and hopefully in Ireland as well.

> Mr Hennessy proceeded to state that he was anxious at once to clear the case of a legal fiction that had been introduced into it by his learned friend when he opened the case for the Crown. He had then told the jury that religious and political topics had no connection with this enquiry as regarded their consideration of it. Religion and politics were matters carefully avoided, and properly so, by the bar generally, but in cases where these subjects were involved, as they were in the present investigation, it was his duty to submit them for the serious consideration of the jury. The whole cause of this ... unfortunate transaction was of a political and religious nature, and he believed firmly that what he might called the crime, had arisen among some of the witnesses they had heard and other persons, who entertained and encouraged towards the thousands of Irish Catholics in Birkenhead, the rancorous and

130 Ibid

sectarian animosities which are so much to be deprecated. The theory of the prosecution was that these prisoners generally, without any political or religious agitation, and without provocation, created the riots and assaulted the police. He would venture to lay before the jury his theory of the case; that the police, writhing under the attacks and charges of cowardice made upon them by the inhabitants and the local press, and being disappointed that the meeting at the institute was not attacked or suppressed, that perfect freedom of discussion had prevailed; that these constables made the most unjustifiable onslaught on the people, and as the evidence showed, beat and wounded his clients while they were running away, not having committed any assault, as the judge would tell them. The police were determined to wipe out the stigma, invited by the press to make a vigorous attack upon the people. Then, with respect to that peculiar-coloured placard it heard about, it was decidedly a party emblem, and a dangerous one to exhibit under such circumstance, and had it been exposed in Ireland, under an act of Parliament passed some two years ago, such a proceeding would have been a misdemeanour. This emblem was taken, and deliberately posted about among these Irishmen, for the express purpose of exciting the national and religious feelings. In fact, a witness said he had never seen any Orange bill before issued by these people. However small the origin of the whole tumult, he submitted it was a matter for their consideration. The learned counsel having quoted from "Roscoe" the opinions of several learned judges on the question, concluded an effective address by employing the jury to dismiss all they may have heard or read of this matter.[131]

131 Ibid

After defending counsels' closing remarks some witnesses were called for the defence. Evidence was given on Mr Fynan's behalf. Two witnesses testified that he had left his own house on the night in question only to help them move some possessions from one of their houses to the other. The most interesting evidence however was given in respect of Mr Smith, the landlord of the British Queen Hotel.

> James Russell, examined by Mr Welsby, said he lived in Brook Street. Remembered the riot. Saw Fynan that night about a quarter to ten, pass by the door where he was standing. It was the door of his own house, 173 Brook Street. Called him and heard him say to his wife, "Take the key". Had some conversation with him. He had been in the British Queen that evening about an hour and a half before. Michael Mullin took him in there. Heard a stone come through the window. Mr Smith the publican said it was, "all right, the windows were insured," and that he knew who had done that. He said it was that vagabond Fynan, the worst member who stood in Birkenhead for nine or ten years. A second stone then came through the window. Mr Smith told some gentlemen they had better leave the house by the back way, and they did so, and witness followed. A boy was present inside the counter bar when this happened. Saw a pistol in Mr Smith's hand when he went into his house. Saw him put a cap on the pistol - that was before any stone came through the window.[132]

So, a brick came through Mr Smith's window and without looking outside he knew that it was Mr Fynan, wearing a bowler hat, with a stick in one hand and a brick in the other, that had done it. The exchange went on:

> Cross-examined by Mr Grove - Judged it was a

---

[132] Ibid

quarter to eight o'clock when he went into the British Queen. There was no reason that led him to look at the clock particularly. Was sure Mr Smith used the word "Vagabond Fynan". Had known him before for about three years. Told him because he did not like to hear him wrongfully accused. Smith said Fynan had done it. Re-examined by Mr Welsby. When he told him what Mr Smith said of him, he replied he had witnesses to prove where he had been all evening.

Mr Curry, clerk to the magistrate's clerk was called. He took the deposition against the prisoner Fynan and all the prisoners when they were examined before the magistrates. Cross-examined by Mr Grove: The magistrates refused to hear witnesses for the prisoners at the enquiry before them. By the judge: Do I understand correctly that the magistrates refused to hear evidence on behalf of the prisoners? Witness: That was so. The Judge: That is very extraordinary, surely all the evidence tendered on their behalf should have been taken, although it might have altered their determination.

Further evidence detrimental to Mr Smith was offered: Alice Simpson being called was examined by Mr McIntyre. She lives at Cathcart Street, and knows Mary Ebery. She used to go to her house. She went there the night after the riots with a girl named Scott. Had a conversation with her about the riot. Mary Ebery said they were going for a spree, and that she intended to go round Birkenhead to hear what the men would say as they were standing at the corners. She also went in the morning after the riot. She said she was going to the police office to prosecute the Irish. She could see every Irishman in Birkenhead with their throats cut. She said Mr Smith had offered her a bribe, and that afterwards he and ten witnesses would go to London.

Cross-examined by Mr Groves. Mary Ebery said distinctly Mr Smith had offered to bribe her to give

> evidence, but she said she would not for a hundred pounds, although she could see every Irishman's throat cut in Birkenhead.[133]

What Alice Simpson's evidence does reveal unwittingly is the depth of hatred some people in Birkenhead felt towards Irish people and that they were not afraid to express that hatred in public.

Mr Smith's evidence was starting to look very shaky indeed. But at no time, now or later, was there any question of perjury or perverting the course of justice.

Unusually, a witness appeared who was closely associated with the Birkenhead police on behalf of another defendant:

> Matthew Jenett was called and examined by Mr Welsby on behalf of the prisoner Buckley. He said he was surgeon to the Birkenhead police. He had examined the prisoner Buckley. He is in a delicate state of health and has been so for some time. He labours under chronic rheumatism. Examined his hands - he has lost the power of his fingers to a great extent. He can only grasp by finger and thumb. Requested him to take off his shoe and throw it at him, but when he attempted it, it fell from his hand. Believes the attempt was a real failure. Did not see him before he went to gaol.[134]

Mr Buckley does not sound like a star recruit to a violent riot. One wonders what the Birkenhead Protestant establishment had against him. He clearly did not represent any sort of a physical threat.

The judge, Baron Bramwell, who at one point referred to Irish people as "savages" delivered a devastating summing up:

> In this country we boasted of our freedom and liberty, and we were apt to talk of the people of foreign countries who were not allowed to express

---

133 Ibid

134 Ibid

> their opinions, but there they were probably ruled by an enlightened and independent despot, and not by an ignorant ... People were not to go and put down meetings by violence, but rather if they were opposed to them, let them go and express their opinions. If those who called the meeting intended to irritate the Catholic population by the exhibition of party-coloured placards, it was a mischievous, contemptible and a hateful proceeding, but they had no evidence of that kind here. There was a story about the placard being printed on yellow paper, but whether that was calculated to excite the people he did not know. If this was intentional, why, then, it was reprehensible, but it would not make the meeting unlawful.[135]

There was little hope for the prisoners if even the judge did not admit the significance of the placards:

> The jury retired at seven minutes past seven o'clock, and after an absence of an hour and a quarter returned into court with a verdict of "guilty" against all the prisoners except Fynan, who was immediately discharged amidst considerable applause.
>
> His Lordship then ordered Patrick Fahey, the elder, whose conduct was not so bad as the others, and whose age was sixty six years, to be discharged on entering into his own recognizance in the sum of £20; to appear to receive judgement whenever he might be called upon, the judge remarking that would never take place, providing he maintained as good a character as heretofore, with the exception of the present instance.
>
> The whole of the prisoners with them placed in the dock, and His Lordship, in addressing them, said he was sorry to have to pass the sentence upon them

---

135 Ibid

which he would have to do, because they were not people who would come there for stealing or offences against property, or were prompted to take that which did not belong to them. They seemed to be men who had been getting their living honestly - at least he hoped so - and by hard work. The very thing which has brought them there, if properly directed, would have been entitled to every respect; but it had not been properly directed, and, with one exception, he regretted to be obliged to pass the sentence he was about to do. They had been guilty of a most outrageous riot; they had alarmed the people there (at Birkenhead), and had been guilty of violence against persons, and policemen who were doing no more than their duty, and endeavouring to keep order. It was a most grievous offence, and must be punished. He would say that if such persons struggled against the law, believe him, they would get the worst of it. The law was stronger than they were. He entreated those who were, perhaps, friends of the prisoners in court, to keep out of such troubles as has had unhappily overtaken the prisoners; and he did respectfully impress upon those whose opinions they valued perhaps more than his, the uselessness of the foolish as well as mischievous conduct they had been guilty of. Such conduct would be of no good to them, but on the contrary will get them into trouble. It was impossible that they could not be punished, for they could not live in the country if such conduct was to be tolerated. Why, then such persons as the prisoners would become their masters, and it would be for them to say when people should be allowed to assemble and, when not, and that could not for a moment be tolerated. They had committed grievous offence, and for a very bad purpose indeed - namely, to stifle public opinion and to prevent persons expressing what they honestly thought. Having, as he said, done this mischief, frightened the people, injured property, and truly ill-used those who had been sent to prevent a disturbance, it was necessary the prisoners should be severely punished. Another consideration influenced him. When people committed a crime so great, they felt that the punishment would be a disgrace in their own eyes as well as to their friends; but unfortunately that was not the case here, for he was afraid, judging from the manner in which the prisoners had behaved, and also the manner in which their companions and associates had assisted them, that the crime was a matter of glory to themselves and with their acquaintances; and instead of concealing what they had done he dared to say that they had boasted of the mischief that they had done - that they had knocked down a police officer and nearly killed him, and also destroyed the serious amount of property. When that was the case - when, unhappily, men did not agree with the law in repressing offences but considered the crime as merit - then the law must step in with severe punishment, in order to make up for the foolishness of those who encouraged the prisoners. it was therefore necessary that he should pass a severe sentence, and he assured them he did so with great sorrow.

The women (with the exception of Catherine Larkin) were each sentenced to six months' imprisonment. In addressing Buckley, His Lordship said he thought of making a difference in his case. He was ashamed of all of them, for they had acted like cowards and curs. They made a beast of the bravery of their country. They had been brave indeed, and Englishman and Irishmen had fought together; but If the Irishman in our armies were like the prisoners, who attacked men in the way they did and then ran away, they had better be without them. Hogan had been found guilty of unlawful wounding but considering his age he would make no difference

> with him.
>
> His Lordship then sentenced Catherine Larkin (who aimed a blow with an axe at the head of police-constable Martin), Thomas Shovelin, Michael Fahey, and Patrick Fahey, to 12 months' imprisonment each. Tracey, Shovelin, Buckley, Gormon, Larkin, Hogan, and Hoare, he committed to two years' imprisonment with hard labour. His Lordship next addressed Henry Lennon (who struck police officer Kearney on the head with a bar of iron), remarking that he might have been standing at the bar to be tried for his life. He sentenced him to 15 years penal servitude - a sentence that caused great sensation in court.[136]

These sentiments expressed by the judge were almost exactly the sentiments expressed by Rev. Dr Baylee and by Rev. Dr Blakeney. The judge's words could have issued from their mouths. Baylee, and Blakeney had succeeded. Bigotry had triumphed.

Something of the Catholic reaction to the sentences can be gathered from the following letter published in the Weekly Register and Catholic Standard:

> BARON BRAMWELL AND THE MONSTROUS SENTENCES PASSED ON THE IRISH PRISONERS AT BIRKENHEAD
>
> Sir, as a man of peace, and in the cause of peace, allow me to give voice to the universal feeling of astonishment with the above sentences have created and will create in the mind of every Irish Catholic dwelling on the face of God's earth. The Irish require just laws and a fair and unprejudiced administration of those laws, and whenever that is the case, no people in the world will be found warmer or firmer supporters of law and order. I have read with very considerable attention various accounts of the fight,

[136] Ibid

or row, or riot, at Birkenhead; and it is very much to be regretted that the Irishmen of Birkenhead did not know that it was unlawful to disturb or interfere with a sectional and party meeting legally convened. Irishmen are as much interested and benefited in preserving and upholding the right of public and private meetings as any other section of the community. But the second and more disastrous fight was a very different affair altogether. In this case the meeting was not disturbed or assailed. After reading various accounts, I have come to the conclusion that the Irishmen, considering all that transpired during the week, congregated in numbers, believing their ancient antagonists the Orangeman would set about wrecking their houses. But instead of encountering the Orangemen, which probably they believed was the case, during the whole riot they encountered the police, believing also the police were aiding the Orangemen. Some persons state it was the police who began the riot and others that it was the Irish. The night was rather dark and hence the difficulty of clearing up this point. Altogether it was a lamentable affair, and as it appears to me, done on the spur of the moment and without premeditation. An unruly policeman or an unruly Irishman might have precipitated the catastrophe. At all events such a thing was not likely to occur again. Every Irishman will admit the supremacy of the law must be vindicated, but he also knows well that in such cases and under circumstances, the law deals leniently with its victims. There is a painful rumour afloat, which I hope is not true, that Baron Bramwell acted the threefold character of the executive, judge, and advocate. The magistrates committed the prisoners on certain specific charges, but rumour has it that Baron Bramwell sent for the Crown prosecutors and made them aggravate the character of the indictments against the prisoners.

... Yours obediently, William Kelly.

St. Mary and St. Michaels, Commercial Road, East. Dec. 29, 1862[137]

137 Weekly Register and Catholic Standard, 10th Jan, 1863

CHAPTER NINE

Cust Complains

Major General Sir Edward Cust refrained from further comment until after the trial. It was not until January 1863 that he addressed his fellow magistrates at the Cheshire quarter sessions. The Cheshire Observer described the speech:

> The Gallant officer addressed the court at some length, but his manner was so excited and his language often so incoherent, that it is utterly impossible to give anything like a connected report of what he said.[138]

Cust made a number of substantive points about who was to blame for the riots, about the conduct of the magistrates during the riots, and about why the magistrates conduct was attacked. Unfortunately, he also at points invited derision and became rather incoherent. It was these aspects of his speech that entered the public memory.

He exonerated the Birkenhead Magistrates:

> He commenced by referring to the ignominy which has been cast upon the Wirral magistrates in consequence of the part they took in connection with the Birkenhead riots... it was only one of the

[138] Cheshire Observer, 10th January, 1863

> remarkable instances in which persons were disposed to accept the opinion which newspapers laid before them without raising any question whatever as to the circumstances of the case. The magistrates were accused of cowardice, and of not taking their proper position. and what were the facts of the case? The riot was put down before midnight without calling in the use of the extraordinary force that was brought together, and the magistrates were literally found fault with, because the special constables and the military were not called upon to do, that which the police of the township had succeeded in doing.[139]

Cust explained why the magistrates were criticised:

> He might state that one or two circumstances had come to his knowledge, to show that the whole of the ignominy and odium which had then been raised against the magistrates had emanated from the Birkenhead police. Before they had scarcely opened their eyes on the morning following the riot, there appeared to be a unanimity among all the Liverpool newspapers, which came to the same conclusion, that the magistrates and the county Constabulary had behaved abominably ill, but that the Birkenhead police had acted exceedingly well. That, his mind, showed that there was a connection between the Birkenhead police and the reporters of Liverpool. The Birkenhead police were at the bottom of it all.[140]

His next substantive point was upon who was, and who was not to blame:

> He next gave a short history of the late Birkenhead riots, stating that they originated in consequence of

---

139 Ibid

140 Ibid

> the discussion, that was announced to take place on Garibaldi. He was willing to say that if he had been a Roman Catholic, he should certainly have felt aggrieved. He did not justify the Roman Catholics, but he thought they had been most unjustly aroused, for he did not think the Protestants had a right to give a lecture on a subject that did not concern them.[141]

He put forward a motion that the Birkenhead police force should be taken over by the Cheshire force. The chief constable of Cheshire, Captain Smith, was ex- military. In effect he was arguing that the Birkenhead Irish should be treated as a hostile population, with a police force appropriate to a colonised people. This was anything but policing by consent.

Whatever sympathy Cust may have expected from his fellow magistrates, evaporated as he made himself a laughingstock.

> To show the animosity that was exhibited towards himself personally, he stated that when on the bench in Birkenhead, after the riots, a parcel was brought into the court and delivered to him, and he put it to one side. When he came to Chester to sit and examine the prisoners, a letter was handed to him, which he put to one side also. When he came to open them, he found that the parcel was made up of a woman's petticoat, and that the letter contained a white feather. (Roars of laughter, which were with difficulty suppressed.)[142]

Cust was evidently preoccupied with the occupational structure of Birkenhead's population, but the nature of his preoccupation was not at all clear, and invited mockery.

> It had a population of 36,000 persons, and he did not fear contradiction when he stated that there were not

141 Ibid

142 Ibid

> more than a dozen persons of independent income in the whole place. It consisted of a population composed entirely of tradesmen and others ... but he repeated that there were not more than a dozen persons of independent means, living within the township of Birkenhead. With the exception of Mr Laird's and the Canada Works, he did not know what the trade of the place was.[143]

What he said was taken as an attack on the ability of the people of Birkenhead to govern themselves. The Liverpool satirical journal Porcupine, commented:

> But Sir Edward properly condemns them. They are, he declares," a population of mere tradesmen." He does not fear contradiction when he says," there are not half a dozen persons of independent means in the place." Quite true. Mere tradesmen. Fellows who work, some of them with their very hands - for their daily bread. They are not like your lofty functionaries who open the doors of palaces and receive the cards of visitors in Royal antechambers. ... Retire, Cust! From that polluted magisterial bench! Herd enough with shipbuilders, manufacturers, and such like! Withdraw to your proud Castle, fill the moat, draw up the portcullis.[144]

The bourgeoisie of Merseyside were evidently not disposed to accept lessons in proper governance, from an aristocrat. His substantive points were lost in the anti-aristocratic derision.

Sir William Jackson was another Birkenhead Magistrate; he was also an entrepreneur, with business interests in Birkenhead. He had become Liberal Member of Parliament for Ashton-Under-Lyne. He gave support to Cust's policy of not violently confronting the rioters.

---

143 Ibid

144 The Porcupine, 17th January, 1863

> Referring to the late riots, he dwelt on the religious antagonism that existed between the Orangemen and the Roman Catholics, stating that the magistrates had to stand between these two contending parties, and, thank God that on the occasion in question, no blood was shed by his orders - there were no wailing widows and weeping orphans - and were the same thing to occur again, he should follow the same course.[145]

Two of Birkenhead's leading magistrates expressed their satisfaction at their policy of ignoring press criticism, and advocacy of violence.

---

145 Cheshire Observer, 10th January, 1863

CHAPTER TEN

Birkenhead's Salvation Army Riots

Birkenhead had its most extensive sectarian rioting in the 1880s, when another lot of Evangelicals decided that the North End needed sorting out. This time it was the Salvation Army.

Now we think of the Salvation Army as a charitable organisation, doing important work with people on the fringes of society, but when it began, it was militantly evangelical, intent on taking the word of the Lord to the ungodly, and storming the citadels of the unrighteous. Which, in Birkenhead, meant the North End.

The Salvation Army described the opposition to it as coming from 'roughs.'

The rough on the left depicted below, is a stereotypical Irishman, one of the Catholic Irish of the North End. The one on the right is an English rough, and they had their part to play in the Salvation Army riots as well.

Salvation Temple[146]

Dixon Scott wrote a description of Liverpool in the early 20th century, and he asked the question," How rough is a rough?" He answered partly with his written portrait of Esther Grimes, a Liverpool Irish slum dweller.

> She lives in one of those blind back courts off Blenheim Street - quite one of the most malodorous corners in the whole of Liverpool's underworld. Her father is dead, and Esther keeps herself and a vile-tempered, rheumaticky old gargoyle-crowned stick of a mother, by tramping amazing distances through the Northern suburbs, selling "stuff". "Stuff" is Liverpool Irish for cheap fruit and vegetables,

[146] War Cry, 14th October, 1882

tomatoes, or oranges or whatever it may be, in a great baskets poised on a turban, perched on the top of her head. Also, so she bellows…. she speaks the hideous jargon of the District, and when the suburban sees her in his own streets for thus fringed, petticoated, bawling and besmeared he very naturally wonders what kind of preposterous nature must lurk beneath so preposterous an exterior.

But I know Esther very well indeed, and I protest that she is not in the least preposterous, that she is not, essentially, anything but particularly normal. She has all the essentials, the right qualities: she is just, she is sociable, she loves cleanliness and good colours, all that she lacks is an adequate mode of expression ... if you could invest her with certain possibilities of dress... she would present, if not a figure of intolerable beauty, at least a very singular vividness and charm ... but as it is ... all the fine human music of which she is so full, sounds fearfully like so much deliberate discordancy. Her sociability, for instance: she is compelled to express that by sitting on a sour doorstep in the middle of a raucous group of messy neighbours. … She is just, but perhaps the only dignified example of her justice that I can produce is her remark (remember, she is one of the most devout Catholics), that probably the folks who insist on leaving tracts for her really mean very well. She is fond of cleanliness ... when one has to get all the water one uses from a little dribbling pump, in the middle of a filthy court; when one has to carry it in a leaky meat- tin, up a slimy stairway to a foetid room; where one has to wash (without soap) in the same meat-tin ... then it becomes distinctly easy to expend an enormous amount of energy without attending any very ravishing results. The result in Esther's case is that you get an apparition so preposterous and streaky that well-meaning old ladies in the public streets are often moved to remonstrate with it on the subject of untidiness.

As with Esther, so with the majority of those about her. They are not plaster saints, and they are not Morlocks: they are simply a community of amiably intentioned life and laughter loving men and women and children, with the average amount of pluck and the average amount of cowardice, all exceedingly human and sinful and lovable and amorous and faithful and absurd and vain, and all compelled, by some strange world of outer circumstances, to spend their strength in a warfare waged on prehistoric lines Dirt, as we have seen, does not mean a love of dirt or a lack of energy; it simply stands for lack of proper tools.

Those clustered slatterns on the doorsteps do not really symbolise degeneracy; they merely emblematize that delicate and wholesome spirit which finds its projection elsewhere in the pleasant devices of our drawing rooms. That ghastly uproar in a place of stench and wailing children simply means that the spleen ... is there being published abroad in the only fashion available. And it is not the fault of these, no in the least their essential desire, it is wholly the fault of the uncouth apparatus at their disposal, that their embodiment of that other wholesome and delicate human instinct - the Instinct for pleasure - should have taken the form of the crude lights and shocks of a corner tavern. But even Esther Grimes might have taken exception, if instead of being handed a tract by some well-meaning evangelical, she had had a Salvation Army band marching down her street interrupting both her conversation with her neighbours and offering an insult with their noise to her place, even her act, of worship.[147]

---

[147] Dixon Scott, Liverpool: Painted by J. Hamilton Hay, Described by Dixon Scott, A. and C. Black, 1907

The Salvation Army typically described the roughs opposing it as ignorant. One should like to ask whether a Catholic Irish person could have had any principled reason to dislike the Salvation Army. What follows is an extended account of a Salvation Army Service in Londonderry in 1882, the same year the Salvation Army arrived in Birkenhead.

> THE SALVATION ARMY. (FROM A CORRESPONDENT.) (Londonderry, Monday.)
>
> The Salvation Army will soon honour Dublin with a visit, and as an experience of it may be useful to your readers, I send you mine, which was gathered on Sunday in this "the Maiden City." "Useful" because some are inclined to suppose that, as this terrible army sweeps across a country it leaves a track behind it of desolation and despair. To such it will, therefore, be useful to learn that it does nothing of the kind. As far as my judgment goes, it affects injuriously the minds of the weak- witted only, depositing in the minds of the strong, nothing more offensive than a strange mixture of the sad and ridiculous, To one who possesses a bird's eye view of the petty struggles of life the "knee-drills" of the Salvation Army cannot fail to be amusing, interesting, out of the common, and, in the long run, more effective of good than evil. I have heard it stated that clergymen of different denominations make a point of preaching against these valiant soldiers as they lay siege to the souls of the towns through which they pass. Now, if I might suggest an advice, I would recommend the clergy to influence their congregations to attend, for seldom will they have an opportunity of seeing so vividly what a travesty of religion is like, what a caricature is made by enthusiasts of divinity, and what an amount of insanity is sheltered from the madhouse, under the garb of a creed. Seeing all this, the contrast will renew

their reverence for truth, it will make them more than ever disgusted with the sham and will dispose their hearts to offer fervent thanks for rational guidance. It has never been a tendency of mine,

I assure your readers before I begin, to think lightly of any form of worship. Indeed, until last Sunday, I had never stood face to face with one which, on the closest examination, could not give some testimony of earnest conviction, and thus it was easy for my liberality of opinion to radiate respect towards church, chapel, temple, meetinghouse, and mosque, and never was I guilty of even an inclination towards mocking or despising any sects until the 18th of June, '82! A light then fell upon my soul, it dazzled me a while, and when it passed away, I stamped and sealed its impression upon my brain. This Salvation Army is, in my opinion, composed of either hypocrites or of lunatics.

Everybody knows that Londonderry is strong in "religion." This creed, that creed, and the other creed are the subjects of murderous hand-to-hand discussions, and religion is a platform for all kinds of public utterances. Therefore it was, that when the "Army" was announced to appear, there was a stir in the place - a stir even sufficient to move me. Mrs Booth, who boasts of not caring a "straw" for her character, is indebted nevertheless to it for drawing good houses. I knew little or nothing of her tenets and teachings, but I knew well she was a violent speaker, a curiosity amongst women, and it was that knowledge which led me down to the Union Hall at 3: 30 p.m. Though it was full half an hour before the time, yet already the people were mustered strong. A young officeress, Priscilla I shall call her; she really is a Captain! - marshalled me into a seat and gave me the word of command to sit close. She is one of the local organisers, her colleagues being, I believe, the other young officeresses who were flitting about on duty, and their trophies of victory in this town were the sickly, ill-conditioned company of soldiers (save the mark) who were collected at the top of the plain unartistic hall. Willingly I would, if I could, hand over their heads to some phrenologist, for to me it seemed as if they all had something wrong in the formation of their skulls or in the cast of their countenances. There were many women amongst them, some of whom were decked-out factory girls, with shaggy locks dangling over their brows, one from whose appearance you would he more apt to expect the corruption of good manners than the refinement of the spiritual essence. By their badges, bands, ribbons, and other distinctive signs they were known to be soldiers, not, indeed, by any mark of supernatural grace. Until the hall could hold no more, the people poured in, and I believe the hall seats a thousand. Every now and again the majors, captains, and lieutenants shouted out the word of command, "Sit close, if you please". Mrs Major - better to call her Major Prim (Trim, had she only been a corporal) - and Captain Priscilla of the pink and white cheeks, large hazel eyes, and soft waves of brown hair, had a busy time putting the ranks in to order, by the time the general herself should appear. It was most interesting to watch the many classes of people packed together as an audience. Some had a sanctimonious, hypocritical air about them; others had a laugh gurgling in their throats; others, like myself, came devoid of prejudice, out of pure curiosity; and many were really in the proper frame of mind to be worked upon.

The platform, too, began to be crowded with the elect; and again, I say I never before beheld a number of faces herded together, with so little character, so little of anything but inanity. There were two men who wore an extra important appearance. They were meant to be Somebodies evidently. My neighbour told me that indeed, so they were, for they came over special with Mrs Booth, and were on her own staff. Perhaps your readers may have had an opportunity of enjoying them as I did. One was the silver trumpeter, the other revelled in the sobriquet of Happy George. Now, the latter took my fancy altogether - more, in fact, than anyone ever did outside of a madhouse. He looks over 40, with a vicious, that would be merry, leer in his small eyes whenever the hydraulics go on. Except an inmate of Richmond, and who believes he is a Supreme Being himself, and Mrs Booth who puts herself side-by-side with the Deity when she does not put herself before, this Captain George is on better terms with all the divine beings than anybody in his senses could be. He started the proceedings by calling on the people to sing a hymn. May I never forget, if I should want to laugh, the funny production which followed. The trumpeter began to blow some dissonant blasts of the silver trumpet, and the shout of words arose, in which sacred facts and sacred names had a handling that deserves to be treated as blasphemy. Priscilla and Prim roared and swung their arms to and fro like distracted pump handles. I was downright sorry for Priscilla; she was so young and innocent looking. but Prim was a tough little body, not calculated to excite much sympathy. The chorus, a jig-like tune, was led by Happy George, who soon could no longer restrain his feelings. Up he jumped, and he actually screamed, "For you there is cleansing, there is cleansing, there is cleansing; for you there is cleansing in the Saviour's blood." He danced his legs wildly about and did everything but stand on his head. Nothing else was wanting to complete this abominable form of adoration. "Adoration!" I blush as I write the word. Between the verses he told us how he was acquainted. Here he would mention the Holy Name with a familiarity not one of us would dare to use towards the most abject menial, and he introduced sacred subjects in a way that first took my breath from me. 0h, the man is clean out of his mind. And yet, no matter how extravagant the remarks he made, the valiant soldiers always reiterated them sotto voce.

Meanwhile Mrs. Booth, foundress of the order, was pressing her way through the crowd. A small figure with not a bad face, good brown eyes, and a mouthful of teeth on show. She, like her women-officers, was dressed in Quaker severity, but was more of a lady and more graceful than they. For a time, she knelt in prayer with her back to the audience, and her offering must have been considerably helped along by the shouting and swinging of arms, and rocking of bodies, and rolling of eyes that went on all round. The people, however, did not aid sufficiently, and Prim pulled them up, telling them they should shout so that the devil would hear them - they should shout the roof off. The trumpeter blasted fearfully, and Happy George was like one possessed. Then a pause, and Mrs. Booth, commander general of the forces, arose to speak. Her voice is most melodious, and her power of facial expression is her greatest eloquence. But she has neither argument, nor logic, nor sequence, nor sense in what she says. She read a chapter of the Bible, with a running commentary of her own between the lines, and in it she proved clearly, to her own satisfaction, that the Almighty could never get on without her. Every five minutes she reached a height, grew furious, waved the Bible aloft, abused it, then hugged it rapturously to her breast, said the Old Boy was there with his weather eye open on us, that synods, convocations, bishops, priests, parsons, and newspapers were all humbug, - it was she and the soldiers who were to work for the salvation of the world. She filliped her fingers at the theologians of past ages, banged them in imagination down on the table, and turning to her brave band told them they were fools (in truth, she never made a wiser remark in her life) but that fools were the proper instruments, and they would always be fools - her dear innocent fools - her dear little Salvation Army fools! And here she screamed out the word "fools" three times, every time more violently, until you could fancy she was on the point of an explosion. This fetched the soldiers entirely, and they nearly all wept - George blubbering and my poor Priscilla like one distraught. Oh, what wickedness, was my internal comment - what a sinful parody 1 Mrs. Booth uses much gesticulation, but it stops short of dancing. She, too, cries bitterly, as she tells many affecting anecdotes of the saving of seven out of her nine children, and of her husband. I don't know how the rest of the audience felt, but I know I pitied Booth and the bairns. She calmly told us that those who do not believe with her are going down, down, down (screams). Her creed is, "A top room in Jerusalem-Pentecost - then helter-skelter, rush into the streets, collar a sinner, and shake the Gospel into him." (Here George chorused 'That's the ticket', shake the Gospel into him.") Occasionally she pointed her pretty hand towards certain parts of the room, and asked the audience there how dared they look into her face and into God's and fancy they were saved. At such an outburst the soldiers would begin rocking, and howling, and sobbing, and echoing her screams. Above all, of course, George would be moved. Slang of the coarsest kind conveyed the most sacred truths, and with metaphors devoid of either beauty or sense, some of the most poetical views of Christianity were expressed. Throwing her arms wildly about, and brandishing the Bible, she yelled that it was a ladder, a ladder, a ladder, and God was on the top. Then, with a seizure like a fit, she announced that she had hold of God, and her soldiers chorused "She has Him, she has Him".

> There is no use dwelling further on this sort of preaching. It was a fearful rant, vulgar in the extreme, not even fit for savages. 'The worst feature of it, is that it excites injuriously some weak-minded persons, and at the end of two hours, about six of the audience stood up to show that they were converted by that special service. There was praying over these, and even my pretty, Priscilla came out with some terrible ideas, with her eyes squeezed up, and a pallor on her cheeks like death. The whole thing amused me for myself, but troubled me for its effects on others. I must not occupy any more space, but I must say I would like to see Pricilla saved, really saved from such a fate. Married, you know, with children looking up for guidance into her gentle face, or else given over to work quietly, unostentatiously amongst God's poor. Hark, the bray of the silver trumpet fills the air. I hear voices, and the tramping of many feet. I rush to the window - it is the Army, singing one of their idiotic hymns, and headed by Major Prim, Captain George, and, and I weep to add - Captain Priscilla. Most beautiful, most gentle! Yet how lost to all that gladdens the fair earth.[148]

When Mrs Booth did try to address an audience in Dublin she was howled down.

This highly literate correspondent of the Freeman's Journal found a good number of principled reasons for objecting to the form and the content of the meeting he had witnessed. His principal objection is probably the lack of decorum and self-control that he saw. He objected to the dancing which he seems to have regarded as verging on the bawdy.

Over the course of the nineteenth century English people had changed; in the late 18th century they were noted for their emotionality. The qualities which were promoted by all the official institutions of the church and the state, in terms of behaviour in public,

---

[148] The Freeman's Journal, 20th June, 1882

were those of reticence, poise and self-control. The English became known for their 'stiff upper lip'. English people looked down on the likes of Esther Grimes because for her, and people like her, much of her emotional life was played out in public. Domestic arguments and rows took place on the street in poor areas. To the middle-class observer this indicated a lack of discipline, an inability to behave properly in public.

Now along came these Salvation Army people who even the Irish were shocked by. Singing and shouting in religious services seemed out of place for Irish people. They thought that sacred stuff should be approached with a degree of solemnity.

The author objected to the surrender of the will of some of the participants, announcing to the world their personal experience of the divine. For him the experience of the divine had to be mediated by the Church, individuals could be mistaken, or imagining things, or plain mad.

For an Irish Catholic, contact with the divine came through the sacraments. The sacraments were rituals which allowed God's grace to flow to the individual. One signified one was a Catholic, by being baptised, by going to mass, taking confession and Communion, by being married in the church or ordained as a priest or nun and by having the last rites performed on one. You did not just shout out that you had seen Jesus.

The initial response to the arrival of the Salvation Army in Birkenhead was welcoming:

> THE SALVATION ARMY.
>
> A detachment of the Salvation Army have commenced an assault on Birkenhead. They have taken up an entrenched position at the Craven Rooms, from whence the happy commanders, smiling captains, and hallelujah subalterns, fire terrific volleys at the sin and unbelief of the benighted town. So far, no disturbances have resulted here from the efforts of the enthusiasts, the populace generally seeming to view their operations with good-humoured toleration and curiosity. A less happy state of things, however, prevails in other

> places. At Sheffield, for instance, the "soldiers" provoke continual uproar, and the other evening they were stoned by a lot of roughs, one of whom amused himself by knocking a Mrs. Dickenson down and jumping on her until he had broken her ribs. From the fact that the miscreant has only been fined costs, it is fair to assume that the magistrates of Sheffield are firm believers - in the provocative powers of the Salvationists.[149]

Given that the Salvation Army had a policy of admitting roughs to their meetings, in the hope of converting them, to some extent they were inviting trouble on themselves. The Army became subject to harassment by young men, probably Catholic and often with drink taken.

> BLOODWASHED MICHAEL AND THE UNCONVERTED ONE.
>
> At the Birkenhead police court, on Monday, before Mr Preston, Edward Elliott, a young man, was brought up in custody on a charge of wilfully disturbing the religious services in the Craven Rooms, Chester Street. Michael McSweeney, alias "Bloodwashed Michael", leader of the detachment of the Salvation Army stationed at the Craven Rooms, said that on Sunday night, the prisoner came to the rooms, and by his behaviour greatly disturbed the congregation. He laughed loudly and conversed with others around him, in so loud a tone as to make it impossible to carry on the services. Witness went up to him and asked him to go out, but he refused, and would not leave until a policeman was sent for. Another member of the "Army", named Clews, said the prisoner entered the room about nine o'clock on Sunday night. He began talking loudly and beckoned some girls to come and sit by him. They did so, and

---

149 Birkenhead News, 18th June, 1881

> he began "giggling" and talking with them, making so much noise that the services were seriously disturbed. It was not the first time witness had seen the prisoner misbehaving himself at the services. Another member of the "Army" said he requested the prisoner to go to the "penitent form", but he only laughed at and made game of him. P.C. 24 (Challoner), said he was called to the Craven rooms on Sunday night and found the prisoner making a noise. He took him into custody and led him off to bridewell. It was a usual thing for a lot of rough young men to assemble and disturb the services by shouting and rushing up and down the stairs and making every conceivable noise. The prisoner said he was present at the morning service and was invited to return in the evening. Mr Preston said the prisoner was not invited to come and behave himself in such a manner as that. The congregation were in a chapel of their own and had a perfect right to conduct their services without molestation. ... Superintendent Clarke said that he had to put a policeman there every Sunday night on account of the disturbances. Mr Preston said that the prisoner ought to be ashamed of such behaviour. It was his first offence, but if brought up again he would be very severely dealt with. He fined him 10s. and costs.[150]

The growth of the Salvation Army movement in Birkenhead could be described as explosive. Within a year they were opening a second Centre in Park Road East, in the disused skating rink near the Park Gates.

> SALVATION ARMY DEMONSTRATION AT BIRKENHEAD.
>
> Saturday last was a great day in the history of the Salvation Army movement at Birkenhead. A year ago

[150] Birkenhead News, October 8th, 1881

Captain Black took up his stand in the Haymarket in that borough, and commenced to play some of the army tunes on the cornet. He was alone, but his playing soon attracted around him a number of working men and others. Watching his opportunity, he addressed his audience in stirring language. His music was attractive, his earnest appeals reached the hearts of some of his hearers, and in a short time a small band of men and women enlisted themselves as soldiers in the army, brought into existence by General William Booth. The Cambrian Hall, in Oliver Street, was taken as a barracks, and in that building hundreds of people assembled every night to carry on the 'war'. Processions also took place throughout the town, and in this way the attention of multitudes of people was drawn to the movement. The number of soldiers weekly increased. Many of the recruits consisted of the abandoned and drunken class, and it is said that the change wrought in the lives of these persons is of the most marked character.

As the numbers of the army increased, additional accommodation was found necessary. A few months ago, the skating rink at Rock Ferry was rented as a barrack, and in that locality, the officers are carrying on the campaign with vigour. In Birkenhead, however, more room was required, and some weeks ago, arrangements were made for leasing the large skating rink at the main entrance to the park. Skating was at a complete discount in the borough and the building was unoccupied. The Salvation Army have taken the building on lease for seven years, at a rental of £100 a year, and it has been fitted up with seats and other conveniences. At the south end of the rink, a large platform has been erected, capable of accommodating 800 persons. The building will hold about 2500 people, but when packed, it is said that 3000 may find room. It was to celebrate the formal opening of this large building, as well as to commemorate Captain Black's first appearance in the town, that the demonstration of Saturday took place. The proceedings were certainly of a very extraordinary character. The army began to assemble in the Haymarket between two and three o'clock in the afternoon. Besides The Birkenhead corps, there were contingents of the army from Rock Ferry, Manchester, Sheffield, Liverpool, Bootle, Runcorn, Winsford, and other places, each contingent being headed by male and female officers, all attired in the uniform of the army. Most of the women wore 'Hallelujah bonnets', and a large number of the men had caps with red bands. Nearly all the soldiers were decorated badges bearing the letters 'S. A'. In the procession there was a brass band from Liverpool, and a fife and drum band belonging to Birkenhead; a number of female warriors carried tambourines, concertinas, cymbals, and other instruments of music. About a dozen women from Bootle formed a tambourine band, each musician having her head covered with a red handkerchief or a piece of red cloth. In addition to the music, the effect of the procession was heightened by a display of flags, and banners. The principal flag or standard was paraded by Private Boothroyd; a tall, muscular soldier, who has served with honour in Birkenhead. The force was in command of Major Taylor, and he was assisted by Captain Black, Captain Case, Captain Falconbridge, Captain Wharton, Captain Hodgkinson ('Happy Johnnie'), Mr W. Gunning (the local agent), and other officers. Amongst those with the Liverpool contingent was a coloured man, who is known in the army as the 'Black Bishop'. He was dressed in a suit of superfine black cloth and had quite a clerical appearance. There was also present amongst the musicians, a venerable character from Liverpool, who at one time was well known and highly respected as a 'professor' of hairdressing. This aged soldier wielded a huge pair of cymbals, and in this way added greatly to the musical part of the demonstration. Upon the procession, which was followed by crowds of people, reaching the skating rink, there was a great rush for seats, and the building was quickly filled. The officers, the musicians, and the standard bearers occupied the platform, which was densely packed There was no formal consecration of the building. Major Taylor gave out a hymn, "All hail the power of Jesu's name" which was sung and re-sung with great vigour, the bands of music accompanying. The volume of sound was almost deafening. The 'Black Bishop' stood and knelt alternately on the platform, exclaiming "Hallelujah!" his face all the time glistening with joy, and his body shaking with emotion. Major Taylor gave a short address, recounting the victories of the Army, after which some of the soldiers related their experience. The officers were received with 'volleys', or loud cheers. Captain Cole (who has been appointed to the command of the division meeting at the rink) and his wife and two daughters sang in beautiful style, the hymn beginning "Hide me, 0 my Saviour, hide". An old woman on the platform called out that she was a reclaimed drunkard, and that she, her husband, and six children were all now saved by the means of the Salvation Army. A male soldier said he had now a clean heart and was living sixty minutes to each hour to please God. About a dozen soldiers were on their legs, at the same time declaring that they had been rescued from the lowest depths of degradation and were saved - not "half saved". In this way the meeting was kept up till nearly five o'clock, the greatest enthusiasm prevailing - the bands playing, red, and white handkerchiefs waving from hundreds of hands, some laughing for joy, others crying, many loudly ejaculating "Hallelujah", "Glory", and other similar expressions.

> Upon leaving the rink, the procession was reformed, and the greater portion of the army proceeded to the Cambrian Hall, where tea was provided for the visitors and others. In the evening, at seven o'clock, the army reassembled in the Haymarket, and again, proceeded in procession to the skating rink, accompanied by the bands of music. The building was even more crowded than in the afternoon. Amid the waving of flags and handkerchiefs, the soldiers sang the hymn commencing "I heard the voice of Jesus say". The din at times was somewhat terrific, but above it all could be heard the voice of the 'Black Bishop' calling out, "Hallelujah" and "Glory". The bishop also addressed his fellow soldiers, telling them how he had been saved about two years ago, by listening to an officer of the Army in Liverpool, Captain Black stated that there was now accommodation in the Lancashire division for over 46,000 persons, and Birkenhead was the 42nd station in that division. Hundreds of people, he said, were getting saved, and if they did not believe this statement, let them look at the platform. Loud 'volleys' followed, the drums beat, and handkerchiefs were waved. The meeting was kept up until about nine o'clock, when the first day's proceedings at the new barracks closed amidst great excitement. Outside the building the army again formed into procession, the 'Black Bishop' heading 'No. 1 Liverpool division'. The soldiers (male and female) sang hymns to lively tunes on the march through the streets and attracted a large number of followers.[151]

However, the officers in the Salvation Army in Birkenhead settled on a policy of confrontation with the town's Catholic Irish population. They decided they were going to march through Catholic Irish streets. The

---

151 Liverpool Mercury, September 11th, 1882

Salvationists knew that they would be inviting trouble for themselves. There had been riots all over the country. Such was the opposition to the Salvation Army in the South of England that a rival army, the Skeleton Army, had been organised, whose object was to disrupt Salvation Army meetings and marches.

Skeletons Attacking a Salvation Army Parade[152]

Brewers and landlords were accused of financing and organising the Skeleton Army. One of the main targets of the Salvationists was the drinks trade, which they accused of being responsible for sin and poverty among the working class. For Irish Catholics in Birkenhead, Sunday was a day many men spent drinking; it was their day of leisure. The Salvation Army chose Sunday as a date for marching. Sunday was also the day when the Catholic Church had its main services.

152 "Thirteen Astonishing Years That Shaped The Salvation Army" Larson J, (2019) Salvation Books, London. Unfortunately, the author does not give his source.

Salvation Army Riot[153]

The cartoon above depicts a Salvation Army riot in London. It was a scene which was duplicated in a number of English towns and which might be anticipated if the Salvation Army marched through Catholic Irish streets in Birkenhead.

> SALVATION ARMY RIOT IN BIRKENHEAD.
>
> On Sunday evening last, the members of the Salvation Army, who confine their operations to the North End of the town, were mobbed by a crowd of roughs numbering from between two to three hundred. The army was marching in its usual style down Old Bidston Road when the mob commenced to hoot and jeer, and not being satisfied with that, threw stones, brickbats, and other missiles at the Salvationists, many of whom were severely injured. Individual members were pulled out of the ranks and kicked and beaten in a brutal and cowardly manner.

---

153 Punch, March 20th, 1886

> This conduct was persevered-in for some time, and soon the road was in intense tumult. The Salvationists were proceeding to Cambrian Hall, and all along the route they were being continually assailed by the roughs. Police Constable Irving, who was present at the time, was unable in his solitary state to quell the disturbance. Indeed he, too, was roughly handled, as also was Detective- Officer Leeson, of the docks, who joined with Irving in attempting to put an end to the riot. For some time, Leeson struggled valiantly to shield the Salvationists, but he was at last overpowered and subjected to rough usage. His face was severely cut and bruised, and he sustained other injuries of more or less severity. The disgraceful scene was not terminated until the Army arrived at the barracks, and for some considerable time afterwards the mob loitered about in the hope of finding some of the band, upon whom to wreck their spite and vindictiveness. This is not the first time the Salvation Army has been assailed. A few Sundays back, several detachments were marching along Bentinck Street, when their progress was interrupted by a French barricade which had been placed across the street. None of the offenders have been taken into custody, but it is to be hoped that only a short time will elapse before they are brought to justice.[154]

The reaction of Birkenhead's Catholic Irish population to the marches, was entirely predictable. The same was happening in Liverpool and other towns and cities. In effect, the Salvation Army march was an unlawful assembly, as with Dr Baylee in the 1860s. To repeat, an unlawful assembly is one where three or more people are gathered for a common purpose, whether lawful or unlawful, which is likely to disturb the peace of a neighbourhood. Birkenhead had a large Catholic

---

154 Birkenhead News, December 16th, 1882

neighbourhood whose inhabitants were likely to kick off if provoked. Birkenhead's Catholic Irish population was like a wasp hive in the attic. The guests might be unwanted, but visitors should not be invited to kick the hive.

Predictably, the only people to be prosecuted because of the riot were Catholics.

> THE SALVATION ARMY RIOTS
>
> At the Birkenhead Police Court, yesterday, Peter Coyle, labourer, was summoned for having assaulted George Gregg, a member of the Salvation Army, on Sunday last. Mr Moore, solicitor, who prosecuted, detailed the circumstances of the riot, which appear in another column, and asked Mr Preston to issue a warrant against Coyle, as the Act under which the summons was taken out, only provided for a penalty not exceeding 40s. and costs. Unfortunately, Coyle was the only person they could identify. George Gregg said he resided at Dock Cottages. He was told on Sunday last to lead the Salvation Army along Brassey Street, and when near the end of the street, they met another branch of the Army. About the same time a number of women, with their aprons full of stones, came upon the scene, led by the defendant, who urged them to throw stones.
>
> The Army desired to go along Old Bidston Road, but the defendant would not let them pass, using at the same time such expressions as "I will swing for you" a crowd of between two and three hundred people gathered, and witness was assailed on all sides, being severely beaten. The defendant used a password which was "Don't hit him, don't hit him, don't hit him", and it was intended the third time the words were repeated, that he (witness) should be assaulted. He was knocked down twice and struck with a stone on the forehead. Coyle was the ringleader, and the mob obeyed his orders.
>
> - Job Hanmer said he was not a member of the

> Salvation army, but he accompanied the Army on Sunday last. They were met by the mob of women and roughs, headed by the defendant, who said they would not pass while he lived. Coyle behaved in a brutal manner and coming up to witness said, "I will swing for you". Police Constables Leeson and Lying, gave corroborative testimony. Mr Preston, trying, heard the evidence, said he would grant a warrant. He said if there was a state of excitement in the town owing to the processions of the Salvation Army, he trusted the leaders would see the advisability of not marching through those parts where excitement was likely to be created. Hitherto he fancied there had been nothing of that kind going on, and if the Salvation Army excited persons holding different opinions to themselves, the parts where those people resided should be avoided. Mr Moore said he would advise the Army as Mr Preston remarked, but he did not think persons in the performance of a lawful act should be maltreated. Mr Preston said the subject was a delicate one, and he did not wish to say more than he had said. Coyle was allowed to bail in two sureties of £5OO each.[155]

In January 1883 Coyle's case came before Mr Preston, the magistrate. What was at issue was whether Coyle should be sent to the assizes, or whether Mr Preston could deal with the case summarily.

> THE SALVATION ARMY RIOTS. POLICE COURT PROCEEDINGS.
>
> At the Borough Police Court, on Tuesday, before Mr Preston, a man named Peter Coyle, labourer, was charged on remand with having, in conjunction with others, created a riot on Sunday, the 10th of December. Mr Moore appeared on behalf of the Salvation Army and Mr Segar, barrister, instructed by

---

[155] Ibid

> Mr Hannan, defended the prisoner. The case excited considerable interest, the court throughout the hearing, being crowded. A large number of the Salvation Army were present.[156]

George Gray, who had been assaulted by Coyle gave his evidence, representing himself as an innocent party.

> George Gray said: I reside at Dock Cottages and am a labourer. On Sunday, the 10th December, I was along with the Salvation Army of which I am a member. About half-past two in the afternoon, I was heading a corps from the Dock Cottages and proceeded into Brassey Street, at the end of which we met the Cambrian Hall corps of the Army. We were proceeding to join together when we were met by a mob of women carrying stones. We proceeded on our way, when the prisoner came up and told us he would not allow us to play the band and ordered the bandsmen to desist. I ordered the corps to proceed, when the prisoner rushed amongst the bandsmen, and stopped the music. He was followed by two or three others, who assisted him. The band ceased playing, and marched down Cavendish-street, and, as I was following, the prisoner said, "Here the b*****d is", and, using filthy language, threatened to knock my head off. Two men came up to me, and the prisoner said "Don't hit him", which remark was repeated twice as others came forward. One man attempted to take the shield from my coat, and at the same time another man threatened me. I said, "If you do, I will get a warrant", upon which I was knocked down, but I could not say who had struck me. I got up again and was knocked down a second time. The prisoner struck me. I was making off to the ranks of the army when I was met by half a dozen men who

---

[156] Birkenhead News, 6th January, 1883

> each struck me. The prisoner said we should stop our band of music going past a place of worship, and I replied we always had done so. He then said, "As long as I live you will never pass here". The prisoner meant the chapel schools, but we had not reached that point. I was cut about the forehead and had a blackened eye.[157]

Gray was then subjected to extremely hostile questioning by Mr Segar, counsel for the defence, who believed that Gray and the Salvation Army were far from innocent parties.

> Mr Segar: You had some sort of a stick or staff with you at the time? Witness: No.
>
> Mr Segar: But you had something you were wobbling about like a drum major? Witness: No.
>
> Mr Segar: Did you strike any of the people with the stick or whatever it may be called?Witness: No.
>
> Mr Segar: Did you strike one woman across the forehead? Witness: No.
>
> Mr Preston: Had you anything in your hands? Witness: No, I had not anything in my hands any more than I have at present.
>
> Mr Segar: Well, they are pretty dirty now, if I may say so. Witness: I have dirty work.
>
> Mr Segar: It is dirty work, indeed. Had you a whistle with you? Witness: Yes; I have carried one a long time.
>
> Mr Segar: Did you placard the town with bills to the effect that you were going to rout the devil out of hell? Witness: Yes; but it was after the occurrence, I believe.
>
> Mr Segar: Did you say that on Sunday next to you would storm the stronghold of the devil?Witness: Not on this occasion …
>
> Mr Segar: What is your occupation when you're

---

[157] Ibid

engaged in the Salvation Army? Witness: Well, our business is to get persons saved to Christ. (Cries of "Amen" and "Hallelujah".) ...

Mr Segar: Did you not intend by these placards to indicate you were going down these streets, and were going to give the benighted papists a jolly good hiding? Witness: No.

Mr Segar: Were you singing a hymn called "For he's a jolly good Saviour"? Witness: That does not belong to us.

Mr Segar: Don't you know perfectly well your hymns are considered very offensive, indeed, to the Catholic population? Witness: Well, I should like you to tell me how they are. I don't see as they are offensive to anybody.

Mr Segar: Now, sir, upon your oath do you not know that the Catholic population have a great objection to your singing these jingling tunes? Witness: They are not offensive to anybody.

Mr Segar: I did not ask your opinion. I don't care two straws about that. I was asking whether you did not know perfectly well, the Catholics of Birkenhead considered them very offensive. Witness: No.

Mr Segar: Do you know that the water committee issued a notice prohibiting you from going in that neighbourhood? Mr Moore objected to the question.

Mr Segar: I want to show he knew perfectly well, and the army knew perfectly well, that the time they were going down the street they were inviting a disturbance in that neighbourhood. I want to show that it affects the question of sentence, and I want to ask him if he knew that the Watch Committee had resolved these streets should not be gone into, and that the Army had been cautioned?

Mr Moore: I must object to the question as not pertaining to the subject in point.

Mr Segar: It is quite clear what they went there

for.[158]

Mr Segar then summed up his case:

> Mr T. Segar for the defence, said that in his cross examination of the witnesses he did not wish to suggest that the conduct of the mob was in any way justifiable, and he earnestly asserted that the Catholics did not mean to say that such conduct was to be justified. The Catholics regretted quite as much as the Salvation Army did, that disturbances of this sort should take place; but he contended that there were circumstances in the case, which explained the excitement under which the prisoner laboured at the time. He pointed out that the Army were divided into two companies, and that their arrangement was to meet in the neighbourhood of the Catholic church or schools, and it was clear that on this occasion, the hymns such as were sung by the army, were objectionable to Catholic eyes. He had looked through the hymns of the Army, and he saw nothing objectionable in them; but he could believe that; if they were sung to jingling tunes, which were more in keeping with a rabble than with an army of saints, such hymns would be annoying to those who heard them. Personally, he could not conceive why there should be all this animosity against the Salvation Army. They did no harm: and if it was intended to convert the Catholics, the Catholics could take care of themselves in that respect. He urged that the surrounding circumstances should be taken into consideration in dealing with the case, and that the best way to do it, was not to make martyrs of the army, but to treat the affair as one of little importance. He maintained that there was no evidence to prove a riot. The Army placards were

158 Ibid

certainly open to a certain construction, for the first placard said they were going to storm the devil. The Catholics, however, should not take notice of such placards, for they did not keep any devils about their churches to get stormed. (Laughter.) Under all the circumstances, he hoped the magistrate would treat the case as one of common assault.[159]

Mr Preston was convinced by the defence arguments.

SALVATION ARMY DISTURBERS.

Mr Preston on Tuesday fined the man Coyle, who had led the recent disgraceful attack on the Salvation Army at the North End, £5 and costs. At the same time, he explained that if any more such offenders were brought before him, he would undoubtedly send them for trial at the sessions. He had been asked by the prosecuting solicitor, Mr Moore, to so commit Coyle, but he did well to display leniency, especially as that leniency was accompanied by a solemn warning which must render any more leniency impossible. In giving his decision, the magistrate made a number of observations of a valuable character. The law, he indicated, was clearly on the side of the Salvationists, and they were entitled to claim protection from the police. But was it, he argued, worth their while to go into districts, their invasion of which was calculated to lead to disorder? He recommended them to abstain alike from practises calculated to give offence, and from visiting neighbourhoods where their visits were unwelcome. It was, he argued, very hard that extra police should have to be told off for their protection, when the exercise of a little discretion on their part would render the employment of each extra police unnecessary. It now remains for them to take the

---

[159] Liverpool Mercury, 3rd January, 1883

> excellent advice thus tendered them to heart. Let them bear in mind that their mission is to promote peace, not to create discord, and that they have no moral right to annoy their neighbours, though they may be animated by the most excellent of motives. If their band is to parade the streets by day and night, there is no reason why Orange and Roman Catholic bands may not do the same. Yet a meeting of the excited partisans of three such bands might, probably, lead to scenes to be deplored by every temperate and reasonable person. It is, therefore, the duty of the leaders of the Salvation Army, who may fairly be expected to set a good example to others, to waive a little of their legal rights, and to defer in some degree to propriety and public opinion.[160]

The account of the riot given in the Salvation Army newspaper The War Cry, however, gives the lie to their protestations of innocence:

> FURIOUS ATTACK ON OUR CORPS IN BIRKENHEAD
>
> From what particulars we have been able to gather of the disturbance ... it appears that the two companies of the army, who have barracks at the Cambrian Hall and at the Skating Rink at the park entrance respectively, were having what may be termed a 'field day'. It is part of the modus operandi of the Salvationists in Birkenhead, to parade some of the thoroughfares in the town every Sunday, singing hymns, sounding their 'war cries', beating drums and exhorting the people to repentance, in a manner that has now become identified with them.
>
> Yesterday, however, they developed a more than usual degree of aggressiveness ... it being part of the programme to make a combined attack on the devil's strongholds at the North End. The Salvationists were

---

160 Birkenhead News, 6th January, 1883

apparently eager for the fray and were inspired with that confidence and martial order beseeming men and it must be added in this case, women - bent on so great an enterprise. They had not apparently, however, adopted the tactics employed in actual warfare, for they did not - unfortunately for them as later events proved - hesitate to make known abroad their plan of attack.

That portion of The Army whose headquarters is at the Cambrian Hall was commanded by a modern Joan of Arc, while the Salvationists hailing from the skating rink obeyed the word of a captain of the opposite sex. Both contingents sported flags and banners, and that of the skating rink was headed by a band of music ... but certain it is that the peculiar school of brazen harmony affected by the Salvationists when they go forth to battle, so far from soothing the savage breast of Birkenhead roughs, has the very contrary effect of swelling their souls to rage and of kindling among them a highly pugnacious and riotous spirit, as will be seen from the facts recorded below.

For some time each detachment of the Army engaged in an expedition against the "devil's strongholds", independently of the other, but eventually they established communication, and coalesced in Old Bidston Road. Up to this point nothing could have been more gratifying than the success with which they had assailed the "devil strongholds". Here, however, the tide of affairs began to turn, and the Salvationists suddenly found themselves in unpleasant proximity to a turbulent mob of street roughs of the worst type.

The latter, numbering between two and three hundred, surrounded the Salvationists, a considerable proportion of whom were children and young women, and commenced to abuse them, jeering at them, plying opprobrious and profane

> epithets to them. Not satisfied with this show of cowardice, they gave free vent to their pugnacious feelings. Slush, dirt, and filthy water were liberally showered upon the Salvationists, all of whom suffered more or less at the hands of their assailants. Stones, brickbats, and other missiles were also thrown at them, and in several instances the injuries thus sustained were of a severe character.[161]

This particular round of Salvation Army rioting came to an end when the Chief Constable of Birkenhead and the Captain of the Salvation Army came to an agreement that they would keep their marches to the north of Conway Street and avoid the large Irish Catholic population south of it. However, in the autumn of 1883 a new and more militant captain came to the skating rink. Also, there appeared to be developing a new consciousness among some Salvationists, that the mission was less to convert the enemies of the Lord and more to fight against them.

> LOOK AFTER YOUR ROUGH BROTHERS!
>
> We scarcely know how best to describe that part of the population which Captains often speak of as "our lads" or "our boys" - the strong young men so often to be found marching in front of our processions, and always ready for what seems to be fun to those who are weak or nervous.
>
> Call them what you may, these men belong to us. There is no question about that. Not ours in the sense of being yet really captured and changed by the power of God into comrades in the battle, but ours in the sense that we exist on purpose to do them good, and that in the enormous majority of cases, their sympathies here been very largely drawn out towards us, so that they believe in us, although they do not believe with us.
>
> What are we to do with them? That is the question. We have raised them, to the great disgust of many

[161] The War Cry, Dec 15th, 1882

respectable people, who would rather they should be allowed to rest, to run riot, to die and be lost in their back slums and drinking shops, than into the streets and hear about Salvation. We have lifted up the standard of love, and light, and hope before these multitudes, and they have flocked around it - not, alas, with any intention of giving up their evil irresistible curiosity to see what all this may mean.

There are many who would our progress stay, and beg us not to weep and pray, and labour for these unsaved masses at least not in the sight of other people, for they profess that they would have no objection to our doing our best for the poorest and worst, provided we could manage to do it without letting anyone else see and hear what was going on.

We will not give them up. That is the first thought that must come to every Soldier's mind. Let the others say and do what they will; let them, if they choose, abuse and imprison us; let them cast out our names as evil, and that continually; but we will not give up the roughest and the worst as long as there is life and hope for them. All through the dark winter nights, amid the wind, and rain, and snow, we will march on to rescue these poor souls by every possible means,

But it is not enough to say we will not give our rough brothers up. We must love them more. To a very great extent our barracks are now crowded with those once rough, now made smooth by divine love; and with others who have learned to love the sight of them. It is too often the case that the roughest find the least opportunity of getting a rest. We must alter all that, and if necessary, we must alter it by keeping reserved seats for the poorest and the worst.[162]

The article betrays an astonishing ignorance as to what was happening

---

[162] The War Cry, 14th October, 1883

on the streets of towns like Birkenhead. The author seems to think the Salvation Army was being protected by their 'own roughs'. In fact, what was happening was that the Salvation Army was issuing an open invitation to have fist fights and worse with Irish Catholics. These roughs would be the children of many of those who queued up to break Irish heads in 1863.

> The Salvationists, or, as many would prefer to have it, those who are opposed to them, have found the Borough Police Court and the officials connected with it, much work during the past few days. Indications of a coming storm were apparent in the early part of last week, and Thursday evening commenced a series of disturbances which culminated in a dangerous and destructive street riot on Sunday afternoon. The belligerents were, on the one side, the Roman Catholics, principally resident in certain of the lower haunts in the North End of the town, and, on the other, persons of a different persuasion, ostensibly friends of the Salvationist party, but who are credited with having been actuated as much by personal hatred as friendship, for those they endeavoured to protect. The proceedings, which have taken up a large portion of the time of the court, have been principally the outcome of the hostilities indulged in on Thursday evening of last week, and of last Sunday afternoon, while the Salvationists were engaged in their street processions, recently extended further into the quarters of their avowed opponents than seemed safe or prudent. Almost daily through the week there have been protracted hearings, the mildest charge in which was one preferred by the police authorities against the Salvation Army captain, who was fined for the second time within a few days for taking part in a procession tending to provoke a breach of the peace. The police court premises and the vacant spaces in the market square have been almost daily

besieged by crowds of persons, who have sometimes protracted their stay long after the hours of court business, obviously for the purpose of discussing the interesting topic of the day and comparing notes upon it. Regarding the action of the Salvationists, in extending their jubilant march into regions where their presence was expected to be productive of butchery and bloodshed, instead of religious conversion, much has been said. About this we do not here desire to express an opinion, as the following reports of the proceedings will speak for themselves. We, however, subjoin a contribution by an eyewitness of the disgraceful affair on Sunday afternoon: The riot on Sunday afternoon at Birkenhead caused by the procession of the Salvation Army through the Irish quarter of the town, was of the most serious and alarming character. At a little before three o'clock there were congregated in front of the Army's 'barracks', the skating rink, opposite the park entrance, hundreds of people all on the qui vive for the return of the procession. A rumour that the Army was approaching caused great excitement, and a rush in the direction stated was immediately made. The announcement proved false, and the crowd returned and awaited the anxiously anticipated event. Meanwhile, along Beckwith Street, St. Anne Street, and Vittoria Street, where numbers of Catholics reside, were to be seen men and women grouped on doorsteps or looking out from the windows. Evidently preparations had been made to give the army a warm reception, and when the strains of the band were heard, the utmost excitement became manifest. The crowds in front of the rink rushed to meet the returning procession, which, emerging into Vittoria-Street, was immediately in the midst of a hostile element. Stones began to fly, and for a moment the music faltered. With a flushed face but with great determination the captain led his forces onward, the drummer waving the drumstick defiantly and the soldiers, male and female, evincing an unfaltering spirit. Proceeding down the street guarded by policemen, it seemed as if the procession would gain the "barracks," now not many yards distant, without any further disturbance taking place; but the mob in their rear were met by sympathisers of the Army wroth, at the stone throwing that had already taken place. A scuffle ensued between the rival parties, and while the police, who showed admirable tact and forbearance, were endeavouring to separate the combatants, somebody in the midst of the crowd waved an orange handkerchief. It was enough. In an instant, yells of rage and hate filled the air, the Irish charged their opponents, and the air was dark with stones. Bricks were seized by men and women and young girls whose faces were lighted up with hate and malice, curses were loud and frequent, and the most savage encounter took place. Close to the rink in a body, were those who took the part in the army, and fronting them were the Irish, who snatching up whatever came to hand in the most reckless manner, furiously bore down on their opponents. For the space of a quarter of an hour, a regular battle took place; those who had been spectators having to fly or take refuge in houses. Then the police, who had been overpowered by numbers, managed to get between the opposing lines, driving the Irish back to their houses. For a time the disturbance was quelled, but for hours afterwards, crowds thronged the locality and a most inflammable spirit prevailed. Whatever may be said as to the right of the army, to thus invade streets where it is well known Roman Catholics reside in large numbers, one thing is plain, the Salvationists if they possessed any influence or respect amongst this class, have lost it by last Sunday's proceedings and the sooner they recognize this fact the better. They have stirred up a spirit it will take years to quell.

THREE YOUNG MEN CHARGED WITH RIOT

Three young men named John Morris, Michael McCarraghee, 33, and Thomas Dowen, 25, Frederick Street, were brought before Mr Preston on Monday. The charge preferred was that of "riotously and tumultuously assembling, with a great number of other persons, in Conway Street, in Birkenhead, with intent to provoke a breach of the peace". Mr Solly, deputy town-clerk, who appeared to prosecute, said he was not prepared to go on with the case at present, but proposed merely to call sufficient evidence to justify a remand, until such day as would be convenient. Mr Preston assented to this being done.

Police Constable 13 (Wylie) stated that about four o'clock on Sunday afternoon he saw the prisoner Morris striking at some people standing near him. Witness also heard him shout out, "Come on boys, we'll rip the (expletive) open". This was after the Salvation Army had gone into the skating rink. Inspector Parker said he was in the neighbourhood of Vittoria Street, along with half a dozen constables, between two and three o'clock on Sunday afternoon. A few minutes reading a printed form of instructions, which afterwards he saw a large crowd of people running up St. Anne Street, down which the Salvation Army were marching. The roughs were throwing stones at the Army and continued to do so until they reached the rink. The crowd followed the Salvationists, and a number of stones were thrown at people who were apparently wishing to be peaceable. He was told there was no authority there but saw the prisoner McCarragher in the crowd that loitered near the rink, behaving in a very disorderly manner, and 'thumping' all the people near him. Witness rushed into the crowd and arrested him, as he appeared to be instigating the others to riot. Police Constable 98, who arrested the prisoner Davin, said he saw him running

> up to a young man and strike him on the face, after which the crowd closed in and bore the young man down. The young man was on the ground and the prisoner kicked him. When arrested, the prisoner pulled a belt from his pocket and tried to strike the officer with it. The prisoners were remanded.[163]

It is fairly clear what was happening here. Under their new captain, Captain Wookey, the Salvation Army had again taken to marching through Catholic streets. This time they were accompanied by 'their own roughs' and a pitched battle had taken place. The police had protected the Salvation Army and arrested a number of Catholic Irishmen who then appeared in court charged with rioting. So far, so normal for Birkenhead. But then - the unthinkable, for your average Evangelical:

> THE SALVATION ARMY CAPTAIN SUMMONED AND FINED
>
> James Benjamin Wookey, a young man, appeared before Mr Preston on Saturday to answer to a police summons charging him, as the captain of the Birkenhead branch of the Salvation Army, with having taken part in a procession of the Army, tending to provoke a breach of the peace on the previous Thursday evening, in contravention of a recently enacted byelaw. Mr Solly, deputy town clerk, supported the information, and Mr Moore defended. The last-named, as soon as the charge was read out, asked for an adjournment of the case till Monday, to give him an opportunity of going into the matter, the summons having been served on the previous day. Mr Solly said the reason why the summons had been made returnable for Saturday, was that all during the week there had been disturbances, and if a conviction were recorded, it would likely have a very beneficial effect in stopping

163 Birkenhead News, 13th October, 1883

> these for that day and Sunday. But if Mr Moore would give an undertaking that there would be no procession that day, he was willing to adjourn it.
>
> Mr Moore said he was not in a position to give any undertaking. Mr Preston: I think that as the town is in a great state of excitement; it would be very desirable that there should not be any procession in the meantime. Defendant: It does not seem any more reasonable to ask me to stop the procession, than to make all honest people take their chains off because there are thieves about.[164]

It is worth reflecting on the significance of Captain Wookey's intervention. He was making a parallel between honest people unlocking their doors to make life easier for thieves, and the Salvation Army stopping their marches through the 'Devil's Kingdom'. He was saying that would make life easier for the Devil's agents, presumably the Catholic Irish population. He seemed to be arguing that it would be absurd and immoral that he should stop his assault on the North End and that an attack on evil would always be the right behaviour. If the law said otherwise, then the law was an ass. The case went on:

> Mr Preston: I think the proposition of the authorities is a very reasonable one, but as there is great excitement in the town and you refuse, the case had better go on.
>
> Mr Solly, in his opening remarks, said this was the first case under the new byelaw, recently enacted, upon which anyone had been brought up. The terms of the byelaw were, "There shall not take place within any street in the borough, any procession or assemblage of a noisy or tumultuous character, tending to the disturbance or annoyance of any person using such street, or tending to cause or provoke a breach of the peace. Any person taking part in any such procession or assemblage, shall be

---

164 Ibid

liable to a penalty not exceeding 40s."

The evidence he was able to call, would show that the defendant did take part in such a procession on Thursday evening last, and did tend to create a breach of the peace, and he was a prominent person in the band, and that he was likely to know from the proceedings of the previous evening that a disturbance might be expected on that evening, and that a very serious breach of the peace did take place. This byelaw was not directed against any band of music, whether belonging to the Salvation Army or not, but was simply and solely intended to secure peace and good order in the town. It did not affect the Salvation Army as a rule in their general work, or any similar society, but only operated to restrain certain acts which they might do, and if a procession was taking place which, from the excitement of the town, whether religious or political, he was there on the part of the police to say that they must ask for such processions to be restrained, when the state of the town required it. If they could not do so by warning, they must do so by punishment. He was not there on the part of the police to condemn the Salvation Army, because the police welcomed anything which tended to promote the good order of the town, but anything which tended to cause destruction of property and very serious injury to persons, as had recently been the case, must be stopped for a time. He had gone at length into the matter, to show that the police did not want to interfere with the Salvation Army, further than was necessary to keep the peace of the town. The chief constable himself had written communication with a former captain of the Salvation Army, the result of which was that they had taken their processions for some time till recently, north of Conway Street, to the south of which there was a large Roman Catholic population, more or less antagonistic to the Salvation

Army, with whom there was always fear of a breach of the peace. That fear they had admitted by saying they would not go there. For a time, they honourably kept their promise, and no breach of the peace of any serious character had occurred for some time.

Inspectors Vowles and Carney and a number of other officers, gave evidence large crowds of roughs had congregated about half past seven o'clock every evening during the week, at the skating rink near the park entrance, awaiting the appearance of the Salvation Army procession. The Salvationists were accompanied by their band, and had a flag, the leader being Captain Wookey. They generally went along Conway Street, up Exmouth Street and Claughton Road, and down Bentinck Street. There had been serious disturbances on Tuesday and Wednesday evenings, and several persons, believed to be members of the Army, had been so seriously injured by stones and other missiles, which were thrown by the roughs, that they had to go to the Borough Hospital. Streetlamps had also been broken. On Thursday evening the procession was followed by four or five hundred roughs. There was a great deal of disorder, the members of the army being hemmed-in by the crowd. In Bentinck Street stones were thrown, so that it was impossible for respectable pedestrians to pass along it. The stones were being thrown in all directions. One officer stated that he had been told that if the Army went again through Oak Street, where a low class of Roman Catholics reside, there was some ammunition laid past for them; and another said he had heard the roughs planning to pelt the Army. Several officers had accompanied the procession to protect it from the roughs and to preserve the public peace.

The Chief Constable (Major Barker) was called to give evidence as to the communications between himself and the Salvationists, but as it referred to a previous captain, Mr Moore objected to the evidence as relating to the defendant. The Major, however, stated that he had had a conversation with the former captain, and as the Salvationists had discontinued going into these objectionable quarters, no disturbance had taken place during the summer.

Mr Moore, in opening his defence, said the case had entirely failed, both technically and upon its merits. Mr Solly had not said what was the statute under which the byelaw had been framed, nor had he produced any evidence of its publication. Furthermore, it was a bad byelaw because it contravened the general law of the land. In connection with this he drew attention to a case published in the Justice of the Peace where the justices for Axbridge, Somersetshire, had bound over a Salvationist to keep the peace, because they thought he ought to have desisted from taking part in a procession, when they knew of the intention of others, calling themselves the Skeleton Army, to meet and oppose them. On appeal, it was held that the justices had drawn an unwarrantable inference from the facts, and that the order was bad and must be reversed accordingly. The whole of the evidence amounted to this, that the Salvation Army, a body of peaceable and respectable people, were trying to pursue their calling in a respectable manner, and that a band of lawless individuals assembled at the doors where the procession came out, for the purpose of assaulting them. He also held that, in escorting the Salvationists, the police officers were virtually recognizing their processions as lawful, and now, with the greatest inconsistency, the police had summoned them. The evidence he intended to call, would show that the members of the Salvation Army were doing nothing unlawful, but that they were perfectly peaceable and quiet.

Mr Moore concluded by referring the magistrate to

the former byelaw, in connection with which he had dismissed a summons, holding that the byelaw was in contravention of the law of the land. Mr Preston said that the former byelaw referred to by Mr Moore, he had held to be bad, because it seemed to be in contravention to the law of the land. He had thought it would be outrageous that a common constable should have the power to insist upon anyone to desist from playing music. But this was a different byelaw, having regard to processions that tended to breaches of the peace and violence, and he held that the byelaw had been properly published and was good. He was sorry that it had been necessary to take proceedings against any persons connected with the Salvation Army, because in his opinion it had done a great deal of good and had been able to touch the feelings of persons, whom no other ministers of the Gospel had been able to find out and had reclaimed a great many people, who otherwise would have remained in their old improper modes of life. He must confess, however, that many of their ways of going on seemed to be extraordinary, extravagant, and extremely peculiar. Notwithstanding that, he regretted that proceedings were taken, and obliged to be taken; but when it came to broken heads and such acts of violence as they had heard described it was necessary, if there was any law of the land to prevent such acts, to put that law into force. The byelaw, he thought, touched that particular question, because there was a tumultuous assemblage tending to provoke a breach of the peace. If there had been no procession of the army, there would have been no disturbance and no acts of violence, so that it came within the terms of the byelaw. Therefore, the defendant, who was the leader on the occasion mentioned in the summons, was liable to a penalty. It would have been wiser and better, and more Christian, if the defendant and other leaders of the

> Army, seeing the state of excitement in which the people were, had abstained for a time from having their usual procession in the town. If the defendant would promise not to have any processions in the meantime, he (Mr Preston), would be only too happy to adjourn the case, or to ask that it should be withdrawn. The defendant said he could not do so, but they would keep out of any streets where there was likely to be a riot. Mr Preston said that had not been done. He then asked Mr Solly whether, if they abstained from going into such streets, he would be satisfied.
>
> Mr Solly thought they must have a small penalty. Mr Preston said he thought the Salvation Army were acting within their rights, but as the byelaw was good, he was bound to inflict a penalty, which would be the nominal one of 1s. and costs. Mr Moore then asked for a case, both upon the byelaw and also upon the evidence given, remarking that General Booth was pretty well advised in the matter. Mr Preston said he would consider the subject.[165]

Ergo in the week preceding the hearing, Captain Wookey led three marches, each of which resulted in a riot. He was fined. The next day:

> THE CAPTAIN AGAIN FINED.
>
> James Benjamin Wookey, the local captain of the Salvation Army, who had been fined on Saturday for taking part in a procession tending to provoke a breach of the peace, appeared on Tuesday before Mr Preston, to another summons charging him with having committed a similar offence on Sunday afternoon. Mr Solly, deputy town clerk, supported the information, and Mr Moore defended.
>
> Mr Solly referred to the fact that the defendant had been warned from the bench when fined on Saturday,

---

165 Ibid

of the probable consequences of the Salvation Army marching out on Sunday. Notwithstanding that riot, they had engaged in a procession, and he would call evidence to prove that a serious riot had taken place, and that the defendant was warned when near the Dock Cottages by Inspector Harrison, that if the procession went through certain streets there would be a disturbance. The fight between the roughs and the friends of the army lasted for two or three hours. He contended that the riots were the direct consequence of the processions of the army, which did tend to provoke a breach of the peace, and this the defendant knew. As the magistrate was aware, there were several persons in custody for taking part in the disturbance, and others would be brought up. The nominal penalty under the byelaw had been inflicted on the defendant already, and he (Mr Solly) would now ask for the full penalty.

Evidence was given at some length by Supt. Clarke and a number of others, the effect of which was to show that a serious disturbance between the Roman Catholics in Vittoria Street and the friends of the Salvationists, was the direct consequence of their having refused to desist from walking in that neighbourhood. It was admitted, however, in cross-examination, that the Salvationists themselves did not throw any of the missiles that had been used on the occasion. Mr Moore, as before, contended that the byelaw under which the information is laid was bad, but Mr Preston, after holding that the byelaw was good, said there was no doubt there had been a breach of it. There would have been no disturbance if there had been no procession, and the defendant had full notice on Saturday, that if the army continued to march through certain parts of the town where they were likely to provoke opposition, there would be a disturbance. Though the defendant did not at the time assent to the advice he had given him to keep

> away from these parts, he had hoped that upon reflection the defendant would form a different opinion, and that was why he had imposed a nominal penalty. On the next day, however, the defendant led the army again into these streets, and a disturbance took place. He could not see what there was to true religion by rousing hostile feeling and bitterness of spirit such as had been roused. The peace of the town had been broken, but that peace must and would be preserved if it was possible to do so; and as the defendant had not profited by the last conviction, he would now inflict the full penalty under the byelaw - namely, 40s. and costs, to be levied by distress, or in default fourteen days imprisonment, with hard labour. Mr Moore then asked for a case, which was granted by his worship. The defendant declared that he would not pay the fine, but, as he has been at large since, there is no doubt, but it has been paid.[166]

Captain Wookey may not have been in custody for long, but it was long enough for him to send The War Cry a martyr's telegram. It appeared along with other stories of the persecution of the Salvation Army around England.

> God Defending His Soldiers at Birkenhead. [Telegram from Captain James B. Wookey, Birkenhead.]
>
> Strange place to write from, a police court, but cannot help it. We told the magistrates on Saturday we could not promise to march out, so we were fined, and of course, refused to pay. Still, they did no take me to prison although I expect that they will today. Saturday night we had a magnificent march; not a stone thrown.
>
> Sunday morning went out again, and with the

166 Ibid

> exception of being pelted just for a moment in one street, all passed off well. But in the afternoon a fearful riot took place. We had finished a beautiful Salvation meeting at the Dock Cottages in the open air, and were returning to the barracks, when we were suddenly attacked by a mob of infuriated roughs. In a few minutes thousands assembled, quite as many being for us as against us. At one point everybody thought we should have to turn back; but no. We never run away! And on we came in splendid style, right through thousands of brickbats and stones. Yes, blast it out all over the world! The invisible hand of The Salvation Army's God was with us, and not a single soldier was struck. The police, the mob, and the press cry out, "What a miracle!" Police wired for in all directions; eighty-five with their chief outside the rink. Soldiers inside praising God.[167]

However, Captain Wookey was to be denied his opportunity of martyrdom. As a postscript to its story on the riots, and the fining of the captain, the Liverpool Daily Post carried the following:

> There was no procession from the skating rink last evening, a telegram having been received from "General" Booth, advising the Birkenhead offices to refrain from marching out for a time, until the present excited feeling subsides. A considerable crowd of people gathered at the rink last evening, but no disturbance took place.[168]

Rather than arrest rioters on the day of the Sunday riot, police took people's names and addresses, and the alleged rioters were later charged and summoned. The Police Court heard charges against a good number of people for rioting. The riots lasted several hours with several thousand people having taken part. There were opponents of

---

[167] War Cry, 20th October, 1883

[168] Liverpool Daily Post, Oct 10th, 1883

the Salvation Army, but also Army supporters. Remarkably all of those on trial were Catholic. The defence was conducted by Dr Commins.

MP. Dr Commins was perhaps Liverpool's leading Catholic. He was a barrister, from 1876 he had been a home rule councillor on Liverpool Town Council, and in 1880 had been elected MP for Roscommon in Ireland. He, of all people, was aware of the sectarian handling of Catholics by police, courts, and councils. He gave short shrift to the attempts by a Birkenhead policeman to dream up the notion of reaction to the Salvation Army as some sort of conspiracy, rather than an expression of outrage to the disorderly and insulting behaviour of the Army and their 'tame roughs'.

> THE SALVATION ARMY RIOTS AT BIRKENHEAD, PROSECUTION OF RIOTERS.
>
> Before Mr Preston, yesterday, in the Borough Police Court, no fewer than fifteen persons were proceeded against for having taken part in the riots of last Sunday afternoon. Their names are Thomas Joyce, Thomas Morgan, Patrick Benne, Henry Atherton, Michael Clarke, Mary O'Connor, Patrick O'Connor, Mary Dooley, John Eceleston, Margaret Hurley, Peter Murphy, Michael Roane, John Morris, Michael McCarragher and Thomas Daven. The last three had been in custody since the beginning of the week, and their names appear in a previous report. The others had been summoned and all were charged together. Other names of those who had been summoned were called, but the parties did not appear. Mr Solly prosecuted on behalf of the Town Council, and Dr Commins, M.P., instructed by Mr Madden, appeared for all the defendants and prisoners, except McCarragher, who was defended by Mr Moore.
>
> Mr Solly, in his opening statement, said he would be able to show that there was every feature of rioting on the occasion, which was Sunday afternoon last. There was a very large concourse of people, and many acts of violence perpetrated. Many people were

hurt and knocked down, in consequence of which some had to be treated in the hospital. What was of more importance, he would be able to show from evidence, that there was an intention to create this disturbance on the part of the prisoners, defendants, and others. Numbers of men were seen carrying stones in their hats going to assail the Salvation Army, whom they actually did assault. After hearing all the evidence, he thought his worship would have no hesitation in committing the persons before him for trial.

Inspector Parker deposed to having gone down along with other officers at about half past two, into the neighbourhood of Vittoria Street. When the Salvation Army band came into the street, a crowd who were gathered waiting for the army, closed in amongst them. At the corner of St. Anne Street, he saw a large number of persons throwing stones at the Salvationists and their sympathisers. A regular row took place, stones being thickly thrown, fists being freely used, and windows smashed. The procession was in some measure scattered by the crowd, but in Back Beckwith Street, they seemed to get together again. It was here he first noticed Michael Roane and saw him throw a stone, and a man struck him immediately afterwards. The two had a regular set-to, which lasted for about ten seconds, till witness and another constable separated them. At this time also he noticed John Eccleston, who gave him some insolence. At the corner of Vittoria Street, there was a crowd of about three hundred people throwing stones, and defendant Banns was amongst them, but he did not see him throwing stones. At a little distance down Beckwith Street, to which he and the other officers went after the first row had somewhat subsided, there was another battle between those opposed to the Salvation Army and their sympathisers. He saw the prisoner Murphy running in the crowd and saw him knocked down with a stone. Atherton was also there and appeared to be one of the worst for throwing stones, and dropped two from his hands when apprehended. The crowd became so dense that he had to defend himself. Disturbances were generally in these streets from 2.30, when the Army left their rooms at the skating rink until nearly nine o'clock in the evening. The other defendants he saw taking part in the affray were Mary Dooley, Michael Clarke, Thomas Joyce, and McCarragher. During the affray he was himself struck five times with stones, and he saw a number of persons wounded. During the disturbance he saw women collecting stones, and throwing them down in rucks, to be thrown at their opponents. He heard violent threats directed by the mob to the members of the Salvation Army and those who were on their side. A number of lamps and windows were smashed.

Cross-examined by Dr Commins: Witness admitted that he did not know of such an organisation as a Skeleton Army; he had used the name himself as a distinguishing name for those opposed to the Salvation Army. He knew that the Salvation Army had issued placards intimating that they were going to invade the 'Devil's Kingdom'. He did not know by this term, the Salvation Army meant the district in which the Catholics resided, but he had seen the Army in the quarters named, immediately after the placards were issued. He had himself stopped the Salvation band from playing whilst passing places of worship. Complaints had been made to him that the Army band had disturbed public worship in various churches and chapels in the town, including St. Laurence's Roman Catholic Church. The Army used both large and small drums and other instruments and carried a banner in front.

Dr Commins: Has any attempt been made by the Corporation or the Head Constable, to get the

Salvation Army to desist from playing to the annoyance and insult of their neighbours? Witness: There was an attempt made when the old byelaw was in force and also a few days ago on the new byelaw.

Dr Commins: Is it not a fact that the Salvation Army have refused to desist from being a nuisance and an insult, to those who do not agree with them? Witness: I have heard so.

Dr Commins: Have you not seen the Salvation Army with such spiritual weapons as this? (The interrogator here held up a stick loaded with lead at the end.) Witness: No.

Dr Commins: Is not this one of the spiritual weapons with which the Salvation Army fight the devil? Witness: I did not notice them; the only weapons I saw used were stones.

Dr Commins: Can you name any who have been wounded except the defendants and those who objected to these rowdy processions? Witness: I cannot say, but I did not see any member of the Salvation Army throwing stones. Witness added that the Rev. Dr Knox had also complained to him that week about the processions.

Supt. Clarke gave evidence much to the same purpose. There was a crowd of from four to five thousand persons in those streets, and stones were flying through the air from both sides like birds. Cross-examined, witness said it had not been complained to him that the Salvation Army selected the time when the services were going on in St. Laurence's Roman Catholic church.

Dr Cummins: Did you advise the Salvation Army to keep out of these particular streets inhabited by Roman Catholics? Witness: Not during the last excitement. We did on the occasion of the first disturbances some time ago, and after that there was a period of good feeling; the Salvation Army abstained for a while from their processions, but they

> recently resumed their marching through these places. I do not believe there would have been any disturbance at all, had not the procession gone north of Conway Street. On Saturday, Captain Wookey was advised by the magistrate not to go into these particular streets in the North End.
>
> Evidence of a similar kind, touching all the defendants and prisoners, was given by police constables 11, 122, and 198, Edward Price, Mrs Leeson, a Salvationist, bridewell keeper Glass, Detective Inspector Moore, and others. Mrs Leeson, of 16 Oak Street, one of the witnesses named, stated that the prisoner McCarragher struck her on the arm with a stone, which would have hit her on the face had she not intercepted it by raising her arm.
>
> Cross-examined: Witness did not know that Vittoria Street and the neighbourhood was called by the Salvationists the 'Devil's Kingdom', or den. They did not go into the streets to make a row.
>
> Dr Commins: But unfortunately, you always do make a row. Witness: We do not go to make any row.
>
> Dr Commins: You do not beat a big drum? Witness: No. Dr Commins: And you do not howl unearthly music? Witness: No. Dr Commins: I suppose you consider the performance very agreeable? Witness: Yes, very.
>
> The trial, having lasted from eleven till five, with twenty minutes of a midday interval, was adjourned till this morning, both defendants and prisoners being allowed out on their own recognizance of £20 each.[169]

If the Birkenhead News was any guide to the opinion in the town, that opinion was turning very much against the Salvation Army and, in particular, against Captain Wookey. He was described in an editorial as a dangerous fanatic.

---

[169] Liverpool Daily Post, Oct 13th, 1883

THE SALVATION ARMY RIOTS.

It is, of course, possible that the Salvation Army has done a great deal of good in Birkenhead, as elsewhere. Its sensationalism may enable it to reach hearts and consciences which would otherwise remain untouched. It is more than probable that many a drunkard and many a sin- stained soul have owed their reclamation to its influence, which has prepared the way for higher forms of religion and morality than its members would yet appear to be capable of inculcating. But when all this has been frankly and fully conceded, it must be admitted that the charge that General Booth's uncouth soldiers are in some cases becoming dangerous nuisances, is not altogether without justification. The lamentable scenes which have been witnessed at the North End, during the past ten days, must be attributed entirely to them. The question whether, notwithstanding the byelaw with which the authorities have been armed, they have a legal right to swoop down on Roman Catholic quarters with their bands, their banners, and their war cries has yet to be decided, as Mr R. B. Moore has given notice of appeal against the penalties which Mr Preston has seen fit to impose on "Captain" Wookey. But there can be no doubt that they have been altogether wrong from an ethical point of view, and that the position will become simply intolerable if it is established by the court of Queen's bench, that they may walk up and down such streets as Oak Street, in masquerade, to their hearts' content. Loss of life and wholesale damage to property, must be the inevitable results of such a line of conduct, as that of which they desire to establish the legality, while it is out of the question to suppose that it would lead to true conversions. No doubt, it is foolish for the professor of one religion to take umbrage at the tactics of the professors of another religion, no matter where the tactic may be practised. But we are bound to accept human nature and things as we find them, and the two awkward facts, which we are required to face, are (1), that religious animosities, ignorant people have always been the bitterest and most easily excited by, and (2) that the Salvation Army specially endeavours to work amongst the lowest and the least well- informed. Therefore, the action of the authorities has been amply justified, and they can be in no way blamed for the deplorable scenes that have been witnessed; it being no fault of theirs that their warnings and admonitions have gone unheeded. The way in which "Captain" Wookey addressed Mr Preston, when he bluntly told the magistrate that he would not discontinue the processions through the Roman Catholic quarters, showed him to be self-opinionated and unworkable. In his fanatical zeal, he appears to fancy that he and his fraternity are martyrs in the minor degree. He complacently compares himself to a householder, compelled to remove the chain from his door, because its presence there is annoying to certain thieves. But the analogy is very defective, the more especially as the Roman Catholics are unlike thieves, and ask not that they shall be allowed to molest the Salvation Army, but that they shall be left undisturbed in their own districts. It is an interesting speculation what General Booth's contingent would think if the Roman Catholics, becoming aggressive propagandists, were to march through the borough, headed by their bands and their priests, singing songs in glorification of the Pope, and if they were to finally set themselves down before the rink itself, with the avowed object of bombarding that citadel. It is possible that this view has not occurred to Mr Wookey, for enthusiasts are seldom able to look at more than one side of a question. But it will be patent to most reasonable persons, and a consideration of it

> will confirm them in the conviction that in a civilised country one man must be content to, as far as possible, practise and advance his religion in such a way that he shall not become offensive to, and a menace to the security of, his neighbour. It is right, perhaps, for such persons as the Salvation Army to be given as wide a latitude as prudence will permit, but even they ought to be kept within bounds which in Birkenhead they appear to have deliberately and flagrantly transgressed.[170]

When the rioters next appeared in court, Dr Commins continued his attack on the partiality of the Birkenhead police. He argued that the role they played made them virtual accomplices of the Salvation Army roughs.

> COMMITTAL OF SALVATION RIOTERS TO THE SESSIONS.
>
> On Saturday, before Mr Preston, at the Borough Police Court, the seventeen rioters, fourteen of whom had been summoned and the remaining three arrested, surrendered to their bail. The charge against them, as previously stated, was that of having taken part in the riot on the afternoon of Sunday, the 7th instant, in the streets to the North End of the town, while the Salvation Army walked in procession.
>
> The evidence of Constable Duckett referred to Mullen, whom he had seen throwing stones and bricks in Price and Vittoria streets. Cross- examined by Dr Commins, witness added that he and the other police had run back the mob of whom the defendants and prisoners were composed.
>
> Dr Commins: Did you ever try to run any of the Salvation mob back at all? Witness: I don't think any of the Salvationists were throwing stones at all.
>
> Dr Commins, on opening his case for the defence,

[170] Birkenhead News, October 13th, 1883

said he did not think the defendants were liable to a graver charge than that of common assault. Mr Preston held, however, that there was a case against them all. He thought they had all been proved to have been throwing stones and taking part in the riot.

Dr Commins, after some remarks as to the part taken in the riot by certain defendants, said he could not allow that occasion to pass, without expressing his opinion as to the conduct of the police; they appeared to have used their staves about the heads of these people, and attacked them, and were to all intents and purposes the accomplices of the mob. Their conduct was simply scandalous. He would say that they did not try to arrest a single one on the other side. They shut their eyes to them, and turned their backs upon them, and devoted all their attention to the other party.

Mr Solly: Not a single officer drew his staff, and the officers are prepared to deny the assertion made by Dr Commins. Dr Commins: There is certainly no evidence that they used their batons, but one of the officers admitted that he laid about him with his stick. Mr Preston: I don't think there is any evidence that the police used any unnecessary violence. Why some of those on the other side were not taken into custody, I don't know. Dr Commins: I think I do, but it may be as well to say nothing about it. Mr Preston: The explanation to my mind is this, that the party now before us were the aggressors, and, therefore, the attention of the police was given to these persons instead of to those with the Salvation Army.

Dr Commins said that from half-past two o'clock until nine in the evening, the mob with the army was allowed to remain at the park entrance throwing stones and assaulting the other party, and not a single one of them had been brought up. He further stated that threatening notices had been posted upon the doors of St. Mary's Roman Catholic Church, and threatening letters had been sent to the priests of St. Lawrence's Roman Catholic Church, saying the buildings would be wrecked, so that they had to be watched night and day. Such things were calculated to stir up violence, and if people were incited into crime in that way, those who incited them were worse than they. He did not excuse their violence in the slightest degree. On the contrary he condemned violence no matter by whom initiated, but common people were not philosophers and never were nor never would be, but he thought that when the authorities stood by and allowed crime to be provoked, they were open to most reprehensible censure. Mr Moore called a number of witnesses to prove that his client, the prisoner McCarragher, had not been out of his mother's house till between four and five o'clock, when his mother roused him from sleep, and when, at her urgent request, he went out to look for his little sister, who was reported to have been hurt and had been taken to the hospital.

Mr Preston, in answer to Mr Moore's remarks as to the great discrepancy between this evidence and the statement of the police, that McCarragher had been seen taking part in the riot an hour and a half previously, intimated that he could not withdraw the charge against McCarragher but must send him for trial along with the others. He then said: I cannot condemn more strongly than I have already done, the conduct of the leaders of the Salvation Army, in going into those quarters of the town which they had already thrown into a state of great excitement and where, from the proceedings of the police on the previous day, the necessity for prudence and caution was made evident, for it was only too apparent that a riot would ensue if they did go into those quarters of the town. To act in this way was, in my opinion, not only injudicious but culpable. I have no doubt that the Salvation Army were and are actuated by the best of motives, but they are acting, to my mind, with a sad lack of judgement. Their object is, I suppose, the reclamation of drunkards and bad characters, but that reclamation can be purchased at too high a price, if the result is bloodshed and the disturbance of the peace of the town. But however wrongly and injudiciously the Salvation Army may have acted, the other side knew that legal proceedings had been previously taken against at least one of the leaders of the Salvation Army, and they ought to have been satisfied that justice would be done and that therefore they had no right voluntarily to oppose the proceedings of the Salvation Army with violence and take the law into their own hands. In doing so they committed a riot, and for that they must be sent to a higher court. I am sorry as well as you (to Dr Commins) that none of the other party are here to take their trial along with those who were opposed to the Salvation Army, but, I suppose, that the attention of the police was given to those who, in the first instance, committed overt acts of violence and for that reason none of the other party are now before me. If any of the other side had been taken, I should have dealt with them just as I have dealt with these.

Dr Commins agreed with every word his worship had said, and tendered thanks, not merely on his own behalf, but also on behalf of the public, for them, as he believed they would go a great deal further than even the prosecution of the defendants to restore and keep the peace of the borough. They would also teach sense to the people who had interfered with the Salvation Army, but who no doubt yielded to their feelings in committing the disturbances, but there would always be people who, from indiscretion and hot feeling, were very likely, when provoked, to yield to those feelings and violate the law. He was sure that the observations coming from the bench, with the weight and authority they carried, would have more effect upon the defendants than any punishment they might receive.

Mr Solly said the reason why no proceedings had been taken against any of the other side, was that a number of names and addresses got by the police were found to be wrong, and the police were now trying to find out the parties. The police had no sympathy either with one party or the other.

Mr Preston: As charges have been made against the police, I think it is well that the explanation has been given.

Mr Solly then asked that the defendants be committed to the assizes for trial, because he thought it would be almost impossible to get a fair trial in Birkenhead with the excitement that prevailed, and the fear there would be of renewed disturbances. Mr Preston said that would interfere with the granting of bail, because only gaol deliveries would be taken at the next assizes. Dr Commins opposed sending them to the assizes. He was sure that the observations coming from the bench, with the weight and authority they carried, would have more effect upon the defendants than any punishment they might receive. Mr Solly then asked that the defendants be committed to the assizes for trial, because he thought it would be almost impossible to get a fair trial in Birkenhead with the excitement that prevailed, and the fear there would be of renewed disturbances. Mr Solly said that another reason for sending them to the assizes was that the jury for the sessions had already been summoned, they came from the very district where these riots took place. Mr Preston was not at all afraid of a Birkenhead jury. He was quite sure they would do their duty.

The defendants were then formally committed for trial at the next sessions, open on Monday, the proceedings at which will be found fully reported in our next issue. The larger number of the defendants bailed out on Monday, on two sureties of £15 each.[171]

The defendants by this time must have been very worried. A generation earlier, defendants on the charge of riot had nearly all faced prison sentences of at least one year. It would appear however that Dr Cummins had been hard at work behind-the-scenes negotiating with the judicial authorities. He must have had great powers of persuasion in that he got the defendants to agree, that the defence he was going to offer was no defence at all.

BIRKENHEAD QUARTER SESSIONS

These sessions, which commenced on Monday, were resumed yesterday, before Mr Clement Higgins, recorder.

THE SALVATION ARMY RIOTS PRESENTMENT BY THE GRAND JURY

The following persons, who surrendered to their recognisance, were indicted for that they did, together with certain evil-disposed persons, to the number of four thousand or more, unlawfully, riotously, and raucously assemble and gather together to disturb the peace, to the great terror and disturbance of her Majesty's subjects, then, there, being, and residing, passing, and repassing in the borough of Birkenhead, on the 7th October, 1883: John Morris, aged 21; Michael Carraher, 23: Thomas Devan, 16: Thomas Joyce, 24; Thomas Morgan, 28; Patrick Banne, 30; Henry Atherton, 23; Michael Clarke, 45; Patrick O'Connor, 51; Mary O'Connor, 45; Mary Dooley, 20; John Eccleston, 34; John Hinds, 50; Margaret Harley, 24: John Mullen, 22; Peter Murphy, 32; and Michael Roane, 26. Mr Marshall and Mr Banks, instructed by Mr Thompson, appeared for the prosecution; and Dr Commins, M.P., and Mr Edwards, instructed by Mr Madden, for the defence.

---

171 Birkenhead News, 20th Oct, 1883

The particulars of the riot, which took place on Sunday afternoon, the 7th instant, will be fresh in the recollection of the public. The Salvation Army, headed by "Captain" Wookey and a band of music, marched from their barracks (the skating rink at the park entrance) and paraded several streets at the North End of the town chiefly inhabited by Roman Catholics. On their return to their headquarters the army were attacked by some hundreds of men, women, and children, who were armed with sticks, stones, and brickbats. These missiles were, it was stated, thrown in showers at the Salvationists, notwithstanding the efforts of a large body of police to preserve order. Many of the sympathisers with the Salvation Army retaliated by throwing stones at the attacking party. A number of persons were severely injured, and had to be treated at the Borough Hospital. The names of the prisoners were obtained, by the police, and they were subsequently committed for trial by the stipendiary magistrate for rioting.

Dr Commins now said that, under his advice, all the prisoners would plead guilty to the indictment. It appeared that five of the prisoners did not throw stones, neither did they assault anyone, but there was no doubt they took part in the assembly if they were there willingly. Under the circumstances, however, it would be hard upon them to plead guilty to rioting. Seeing, however, that the prisoners were the only persons who were injured, and beyond the disturbance of the public peace, he apprehended no very serious harm had been done. He had advised them to plead guilty, to throw themselves on the mercy of the court, and acknowledge they had done wrong. There was an illegal assemblage, if not a riot -some of the prisoners being rioters - and it would be hard to spend the whole of the day in finding out who were the rioters, and who were not.

... The Recorder said he had read the depositions

very carefully, and as the prisoners had thrown themselves on the mercy of the court, he thought it was better to leave the matter there, because any statement made on the one side, might lead to statements on the other. Addressing the prisoners, the learned recorder then said they had pleaded guilty to riot on the advice of their counsel, and he could not hesitate to say it was very good advice. He (the recorder) had read the depositions very carefully, and in his opinion a riot took place, and there was no doubt that all the prisoners were there and took a part in it. It was also beyond doubt, in his opinion, that if they had been tried by a jury, they would have been found guilty, and if they had done so, after a long trial, he should have been bound to send them for a term of imprisonment. He said that, to show the prisoners what good advice their counsel had given them. The peace of the borough must be kept, and the prisoners must not go away with any supposition, notion, or idea that they could break the peace of the district with impunity. He was going to deal leniently with them on this occasion; but they must bear in mind that taking part in any future riot would bear fruit. He was going to bind them over to come up for judgement when called upon. If they took part in any future riot or unlawful assembly, or did anything in any way tending to a breach of the peace in connection with this matter, they would have to come again before him, and he should then pass judgement upon their present plea of guilty; but if they behaved well in future, they would hear no more of the matter. He would not say a single word to justify or excuse their conduct, but he was free to admit that they might have received some provocation. What he had to consider, and what the grand jury had to consider, and what the petty jury would have had to consider if the prisoners had been brought before them, was the absolute necessity of maintaining the peace of the borough. The grand jury, with that view, had made a presentment to which he should call the attention of the proper authorities. The presentment was, "The grand jury desire to make presentment that, in their opinion, it is desirable that the by-law made on the 6th June, 1883, by the town council with reference to processions in the public streets, should be enforced as far as possible, in order that the peace of the borough may not be disturbed." The byelaw referred to was as follows: "There shall not take place in any public street within the borough, any procession of a noisy or tumultuous character, tending to the obstruction or annoyance to the public using such street, or tending to cause or provoke a breach of the peace. Any person taking part in any such procession or assembly shall be liable to a penalty not exceeding 40s." Now, that was the byelaw, and that was the presentment of the grand jury, and he should take care that it went before the authorities, who, he had not the least doubt, would act in a right, and proper, and vigorous way upon it. What they all wanted was that those who entertained one view, and that the Salvation Army, who entertained another view, should be able to live in the borough in peace, without committing any breach of the law, because they knew that the borough was big enough for both of them. If the Salvation Army abstained from having any procession, or any assembly of a noisy or tumultuous character, on the one hand, and if the prisoners and others also abstained, on the other hand, from interfering with them - so long as they did not commit a breach of the peace - then there would be peace in the borough, and they might go on with their work and enjoy their opinions without any interference from the Salvation Army. The Salvation Army might also go on holding their views without any interference, and in this way the peace of the

> borough would be preserved. The great point was that the peace of the borough must be kept; and if rioting took place again, and the prisoners took part in it, they would be brought up for judgement.
>
> The prisoners were then bound in their own recognisance, in the sum of £25 each, to come up for judgement if called upon. They were afterwards discharged.[172]

The contrast with the treatment of the Garibaldi rioters could not be greater. In 1863 the town authorities had insisted on the right to insult Catholics, describing it as 'free speech'. In 1883 the courts and informed opinion insisted that it was the right of Catholics not to be insulted. The verdict met with the approval of The Birkenhead News:

> THE SALVATION ARMY RIOT
>
> Most dispassionate persons will approve of the way in which the recorder treated the seventeen persons who pleaded guilty to having been concerned in the recent rioting at the North End. They were not deserving of severe punishment, and no doubt their counsel, Dr Commins, persuaded them to admit their culpableness confident, in his own mind, that they would be treated pretty much as they were. It might have been better if the case had been sifted from top to bottom, as in that event the proceedings would have possessed a seriousness which, as it was, did not attach to them. The recorder, however, in discharging them on their own recognizance to come up for judgement when called upon, addressed them with a degree of impressiveness and solemnity calculated to remove any idea that they had committed a trivial offence which, if they were again aggravated as they had undoubtedly been, they might repeat with impunity. He very plainly stated that if their quarters were

172 Liverpool Mercury, 25th Oct, 1883

further invaded by the Salvation Army, and they in any way retaliated, they would undoubtedly receive severe punishment at his hands. The Salvation Army has been mainly responsible for the miserable disturbances which have kept the North End in such a turmoil. It is, therefore, gratifying that the proceedings of the court of quarter sessions did not begin and end with admonitions to the Roman Catholic rioters, who were the only ones the police had been able to discover, though there had admittedly been Salvationist rioters also. The grand jury made a very strong presentment, which was warmly endorsed by the recorder, that the byelaw empowering the police to deal with disorderly processions should be strictly carried out. The hands of the authorities will be greatly strengthened by this. In the past the police and the watch committee have, no doubt, largely been held in check by the sentimentalists who, believing the Salvation Army to be doing a great work, would allow it to make itself master of the public thoroughfares as well as its own quarters, where, of course, not even the Roman Catholics themselves have not the slightest wish to interfere with it. It remains to be seen whether all parties will consent to profit by the lessons which have been given. If the Army's captains are impracticable and insist on courting attack, they will incur a serious moral responsibility, as well as invite the head constable to restrain them as far as may be by legal means. It really rests with them whether we are to have peace and quietness or disorder and ruffianism, for they can, if they like, keep to districts where they may play and sing to their hearts' content without being molested, but it is not always possible for impulsive Irish Roman Catholics to restrain their tempers when they imagine that they and their religion are being insulted.[173]

It had taken nearly forty years, but by the early 1880s the era of organised assaults on the Catholic population of Birkenhead had come to an end. This is not to say that that population had ceased to be victimised. The North End continued to be overpoliced. Expressions of religious hatred, such as Orange marches, carried on. The last Orange march down Borough Road took place in the closing years of the twentieth century. Twentieth century riots had poverty rather than religion at their roots.

173 Birkenhead News, Sat Oct 27th, 1883

About the Author

Kevin McCusker was born and brought up in Birkenhead. He attended St Werburgh's School and Church, going on to study at St Anselm's College. He was awarded an Upper Second Class Honours degree in History and Philosophy followed by a First Class Honours degree in History at Bangor University. After thirty-seven years working in further education in Telford, Shropshire, he went on to be awarded the degree of Master of Research from the University of Liverpool in 2016. His dissertation topic was the Birkenhead Garibaldi riots of 1862. The only other material on the riots was written by Frank Neal. His version is seen as somewhat flawed, as it places much certainty on the accuracy of events according to the police account; something we now know must be viewed with a degree of scepticism.

Printed in Great Britain
by Amazon